SHORT WALKS
HADRIAN'S WALL

by Mark Richards

CICERONE

CONTENTS

Using this guide. 4
Route summary table 6
Map key. 7
Introduction. 9
  The building of Hadrian's Wall. 9
  Walking in Hadrian's Wall country 10
  Bases and where to stay 11
  Travel 11

The walks

1. Walton and Cam Beck 13
2. Lanercost Priory. 19
3. Combcrag Gorge. 25
4. Birdoswald and Gilsland Spa 31
5. Nine Nicks of Thirlwall. 37
6. Great Chesters 43
7. Cawfield Crags 47
8. Winshield Crags 51
9. Sycamore Gap. 55
10. Vindolanda and Barcombe Hill 61
11. Housesteads 67
12. Sewingshields Crags 73
13. Limestone Corner. 79
14. Heavenfield. 83
15. Portgate and Halton 89

Useful information. 94

USING THIS GUIDE

Routes in this book

In this book you will find a selection of easy or moderate walks suitable for almost everyone, including casual walkers and families with children, or for when you only have a short time to fill. The routes have been carefully chosen to allow you to explore the area and its attractions. All of the routes are circular. Although there may be some climbs there is no challenging terrain, but do bear in mind that conditions can sometimes be wet or muddy underfoot. A route summary table is included on page 6 to help you choose the right walk.

Clothing and footwear

You won't need any special equipment to enjoy these walks. The weather in Britain can be changeable, so choose clothing suitable for the season and wear or carry a waterproof jacket. For footwear, comfortable walking boots or trainers with a good grip are best. A small rucksack for drinks, snacks and spare clothing is useful. See www.adventuresmart.uk.

Walk descriptions

At the beginning of each walk you'll find all the information you need:

• start/finish location, with postcode and a what3words address to help you find it
• parking and transport information, estimated walking time, total distance and climb
• details of public toilets available along the route and where you can get refreshments
• a summary of the key highlights of the walk and what you might see

Timings given are the time to complete the walk at a reasonable walking pace. Allow extra time for extended stops or if walking with children.

The route is described in clear, easy-to-follow directions, with each waypoint marked on an accompanying map extract. It's a good idea to read the whole of the route instructions before setting out, so that you know what to expect.

Maps, GPX files and what3words

Extracts from the OS 1:25,000 map accompany each route. GPX files for all the walks in this book are available to download at www.cicerone.co.uk/1157/gpx.

What3words is a free smartphone app which identifies every 3m square of the globe with a unique three-word address, e.g. ///destiny.cafe.sonic. For more information see https://what3words.com/products/what3words-app.

Walking with children

Even young children can be surprisingly strong walkers, but every family is different and you may need to adapt the timings given in this book to take that into account. Make sure you go at the pace of the slowest member and choose a walk with an exciting objective in mind, such as a cave, waterfall or picnic spot. Many of the walks can be shortened to suit – suggestions are included at the end of the route description.

Dogs

Sheep or cattle may be found grazing on a number of these walks. Keep dogs under control at all times so that they don't scare or disturb livestock or wildlife. Cattle, particularly cows with calves, may very occasionally pose a risk to walkers with dogs. If you ever feel threatened by cattle, you should let go of your dog's lead and let it run free.

Enjoying the countryside responsibly

Enjoy the countryside and treat it with respect to protect our natural environments. Stick to footpaths and take your litter home with you. When driving, slow down on rural roads and park considerately, or better still use public transport. For more details check out www.gov.uk/countryside-code.

The Countryside Code

Respect everyone

- be considerate to those living in, working in and enjoying the countryside
- leave gates and property as you find them
- do not block access to gateways or driveways when parking
- be nice, say hello, share the space
- follow local signs and keep to marked paths unless wider access is available

Protect the environment

- take your litter home – leave no trace of your visit
- do not light fires and only have BBQs where signs say you can
- always keep dogs under control and in sight
- dog poo – bag it and bin it – any public waste bin will do
- care for nature – do not cause damage or disturbance

Enjoy the outdoors

- check your route and local conditions
- plan your adventure – know what to expect and what you can do
- enjoy your visit, have fun, make a memory

ROUTE SUMMARY TABLE

WALK NAME	START POINT	TIME	DISTANCE
1. Walton and Cam Beck	Walton	2¼hr	5.5km (3½ miles)
2. Lanercost Priory	Lanercost Bridge	2¼hr	5km (3¼ miles)
3. Combcrag Gorge	Banks Turret	2¼hr	5.5km (3½ miles)
4. Birdoswald and Gilsland Spa	Gilsland	3hr	8.5km (5¼ miles)
5. Nine Nicks of Thirlwall	Walltown Country Park	1¾hr	4.5km (2¾ miles)
6. Great Chesters	Cawfields Quarry	2¾hr	7.5km (4½ miles)
7. Cawfield Crags	Cawfields Quarry	1½hr	4km (2½ miles)
8. Winshield Crags	Steel Rigg	1½hr	5km (3 miles)
9. Sycamore Gap	Steel Rigg	1¾hr	5.5km (3½ miles)
10. Vindolanda and Barcombe Hill	Bardon Mill	3hr	7.5km (4¾ miles)
11. Housesteads	Housesteads	3hr	7.5km (4¾ miles)
12. Sewingshields Crags	Housesteads	4hr	10.5km (6½ miles)
13. Limestone Corner	Brocolitia	2½hr	6.5km (4 miles)
14. Heavenfield	Wall village	3hr	8km (5 miles)
15. Portgate and Halton	Portgate, near Corbridge	3hr	8km (5 miles)

HIGHLIGHTS

Picturesque village and a
lovely wooded valley

Scenic pastures and
priory ruins

River, dramatic gorge and
Roman turrets

Fine stretches of Wall,
a Roman fort and milecastle

Scenic Wall section and
impressive crags

Roman cavalry fort and
quiet valley

Handsome section of Wall,
pasture and streamside

Highest point on frontier
with great views

Switchback ridge with
iconic tree

Famous Roman fort and
a hill with views

Fine section of Wall and
showpiece fort

Whin Sill, milecastle and
great views

Northernmost point
on the frontier

Iron age settlement,
battlefield

Pastures, green lanes
and wild wood

SYMBOLS USED ON ROUTE MAPS

(S) Start point

(F) Finish point

(SF) Start and finish
at the same place

4→ Waypoint

~ Route line

MAPPING IS SHOWN AT A SCALE OF 1:25,000

0 KM   0.25   0.5

0 miles   0.25

DOWNLOADED THE GPX FILES FREE AT

www.cicerone.co.uk/1157/GPX

Walkers approaching Milking Gap (Walk 9)

INTRODUCTION

The Roman frontier, now 1900 years old, may be largely a ghost over much of its original course, but its impact on the mind's eye remains powerful and compelling. Running 80 Roman miles (120km) coast to coast from the Solway Coast in the west to Wallsend near Newcastle upon Tyne in the east, Hadrian's Wall was an impressive feat of engineering. Visual reconstructions show a tall, crenellated, stone barrier striding the countryside and stretching along the brink of crags on the Whin Sill scarp, with ditches, forts and watchtowers. The remnants of the stone wall and its fortifications are still visible in many places and form the basis of some exciting discovery walks.

Hadrian's Wall country has long held a special attraction for visitors, beginning in the Victorian age when scholarly antiquarians and amateur historians sought to find what remained of this unique monument. In 1987 the Wall was designated a UNESCO World Heritage Site, bringing a world-wide audience of curious travellers and walkers.

The building of Hadrian's Wall

Construction of the Wall began around AD121 under the instructions of Emperor Hadrian. The first incarnation of the Wall took eight years to build. Approximately every five miles along the Wall there was a garrison fort, with a patrol base milecastle every mile and two turret towers every third of a mile in between. To the north there was a deep ditch with an upcast mound. The frontier was completed by a double bank and ditch feature known as the vallum, which defined the military zone to the south.

The pre-existing Stanegate, between Carlisle and Corbridge, served as a supply road. After the Romans abandoned the Antonine Wall in Scotland some 60 years later, they built a Military Way close to Hadrian's Wall to speed movement. The Wall served to contain the most economically valuable part of Britannia and to bring native tribes under strict Roman jurisdiction, while allowing controlled movement and trade. It was abandoned around AD410.

The largest Roman archaeological feature in Britain, Hadrian's Wall remains standing in some sections, and in many places the remnants of turrets and milecastles and the vallum are still visible. The remains of forts at Housesteads and Birdoswald and museums at Vindolanda and Chesters give a fascinating insight into life in this outpost of the Roman Empire.

Roman altar with Scots Blackface ewe and lamb (Walk 6)

Walking in Hadrian's Wall country

The 84-mile Hadrian's Wall Path National Trail runs the length of the Wall, but even if a multi-day trek is not for you, you can still experience some parts of it. This guide draws you into very best of the frontier landscape, each walk revealing the beauty and drama of the region and highlighting heritage from the classical age when Romans garrisoned the forts and all roads led to Rome.

All walks are circular and take from 1½ to 4hr to complete, and while some involve a little ascent and descent, they are never too taxing. They are the perfect introduction to the Roman Wall in its historic setting and to this wonderful landscape with far-ranging views.

When visiting the Roman Wall or following any of the routes in this guide, please do not walk on top of the Wall itself. It will always be vulnerable to damage by overenthusiastic visitors. Always walk beside archaeological remains, not on them. It is also important to remember this is an agricultural landscape with cattle and sheep at pasture, so if you are walking with dogs keep them under close control on a lead.

Bases and where to stay

Accommodation can be found in the narrow band of country between Carlisle and Newcastle. Brampton, Haltwhistle, Hexham and Corbridge all make good bases from which to access the walks in this guide, and there is a diverse selection of other places to stay in the countryside round about.

Travel

Trains along the Tyne Valley Line link Newcastle, Hexham and Carlisle, calling at Haydon Bridge, Bardon Mill, Haltwhistle and Brampton. Buses are mostly operated by Go North East. The most useful is the popular AD122 bus which in summer (July–October) runs hourly between Hexham and Haltwhistle along the line of the Military Road (B6318). This service stops at or near the start of several walks in this book.

For car drivers the A69 forms the primary route to Hadrian's Wall Country. Walks 1, 2 and 3 are most efficiently approached from Brampton. The other walks (apart from Walk 10 which uses the rail service) are best accessed off the Military Road between Portgate (Corbridge) and Greenhead.

Hadrian's Wall is 11 courses high along Walltown Crags (Walk 5)

Walton parish church

WALK 1

Walton and Cam Beck

Start/finish	*Walton village green*
Locate	*CA8 2DH ///traders.moral.revisits*
Cafes/pubs	*Reading Room cafe and Old Vicarage Brewery for home brew, beverages and evening meals*
Transport	*No buses*
Parking	*Grass and verge parking in the centre of the village*
Toilets	*No public toilets on route*

This is a charming rural stroll, largely through pasture and along farm tracks. Walton, arranged around its tree-shaded green, sets the tone of the walk. The woods at Castlesteads and above Cam Beck are full of bluebells early in the year.

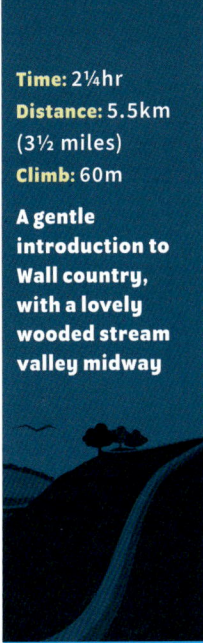

Time: 2¼hr
Distance: 5.5km (3½ miles)
Climb: 60m

A gentle introduction to Wall country, with a lovely wooded stream valley midway

Castlesteads

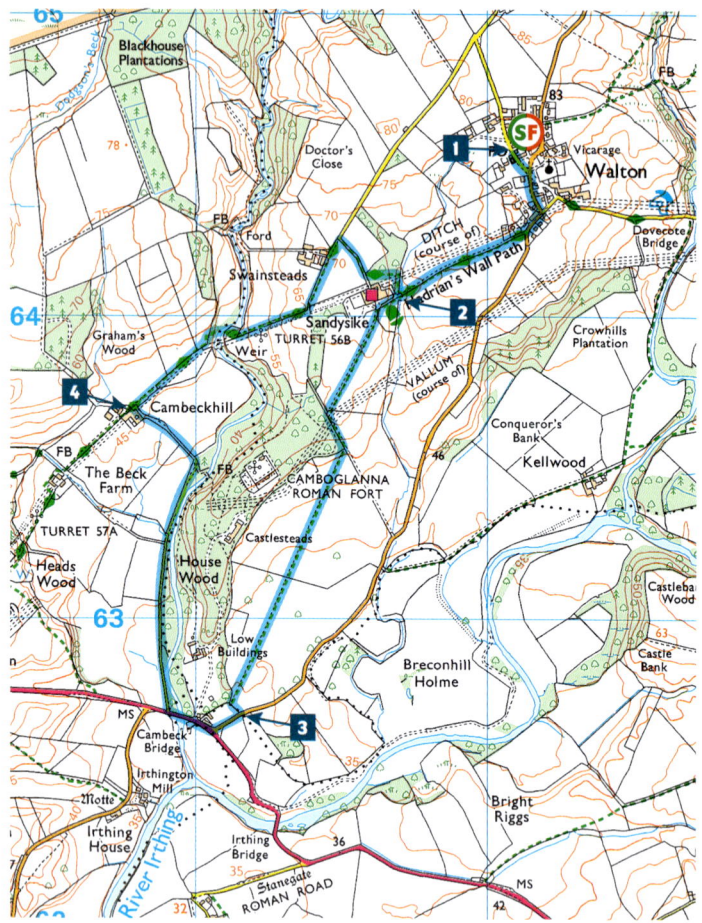

1 From the Old Reading Room cafe follow the road south past the bus shelter, turning right at the T-junction to connect with the waymarks of the **Hadrian's Wall Path** National Trail. As the road leaves the village westwards follow signs through a kissing-gate into a pasture and continue along the hedgeside track.

Walton's tree-lined green

The village of Walton is delightfully and irregularly set out around an open tree-lined green, like a gathering of friends. The village name is Anglo-Saxon, meaning 'farm on Hadrian's Wall', coined when the ruined stone frontier would still have been visible.

2 Go through a gate to the left of the National Trail kissing-gate, and at the next gate follow the track up towards the garden wall of **Sandysike**. Turn left across the cattle-grid, follow the open track across a field, through a gate then alongside woodland. Stay with the woodside track through a kissing-gate and cross the open pasture, commonly grazed by sheep. The big house to the right is **Castlesteads**. The footpath crosses a fence-stile midway across and comes eventually via another stile to the road.

> *ⓘ During the many phases of the ice age, great glaciers swept west across this landscape sculpting the surface features we see today.*

Castlesteads

Bluebells in Castlesteads woodland

Castlesteads is a grand red sandstone house set in bluebell-rich woodland and can be seen clearly from the footpath crossing the park. Its hidden walled garden sits on the site of the Roman fort of Camboglanna, meaning 'the curved bank above the crooked stream'. The fort and the Wall were separated by Cam Beck, which formed a defensive position for the garrison in this, the more disturbed, western sector of the frontier.

Cam Beck weir

Tea room in Walton

3 Turn right and at the junction go right, passing the row of cottages. Cross the road bridge (be aware of oncoming traffic), then turn right and walk along the farm road to **Cambeck Hill Farm** initially close to wooded Cam Beck. Pass the farm buildings and turn right through a kissing-gate in the fence to rejoin the National Trail.

4 Continue through the pasture via three kissing-gates into the woods above **Cam Beck**. Descend to cross a purpose-built footbridge where for centuries there was only a ford. Excavations in 2021 revealed a lookout tower on the west bank. The curved weir is set precisely where the stone curtain wall spanned the beck. Follow the slabbed path, leaving the woodland at a kissing-gate into pasture, walk up alongside the shallow mound of the Roman Wall's north ditch to a signpost and fence gap. Bear left through the field-gate. Keep the hedge on your left, passing Swainsteads farm to reach a kissing-gate by a cattle-grid. Turn right along the access lane to **Sandysike**. Pass through a kissing-gate on the left into woodland, then through another kissing-gate to retrace your outward route back to **Walton**.

The remains of Priory Garth gatehouse

WALK 2
Lanercost Priory

Time: 2¼hr
Distance: 5km
(3¼ miles)
Climb: 90m

A lovely wander through rolling countryside to find the first hints of the frontier

Start/finish	*Picnic site by Lanercost Bridge*
Locate	*CA8 2HQ ///inert.holidays.cured*
Cafes/pubs	*Lanercost tea room and several in nearby Brampton (off route), plus a trailside refreshment cabin (honesty box) at Haytongate*
Transport	*No buses*
Parking	*Beside Lanercost Bridge and within the Priory Garth (free)*
Toilets	*No public toilets on route*

A lovely stroll that connects with the line of the frontier through a rolling pastoral landscape. After leaving the Roman Wall, the walk returns to Lanercost and gently onwards along the banks of the River Irthing. Allow some extra time to visit the peaceful priory ruins.

Looking east along the National Trail at Burtholme Beck

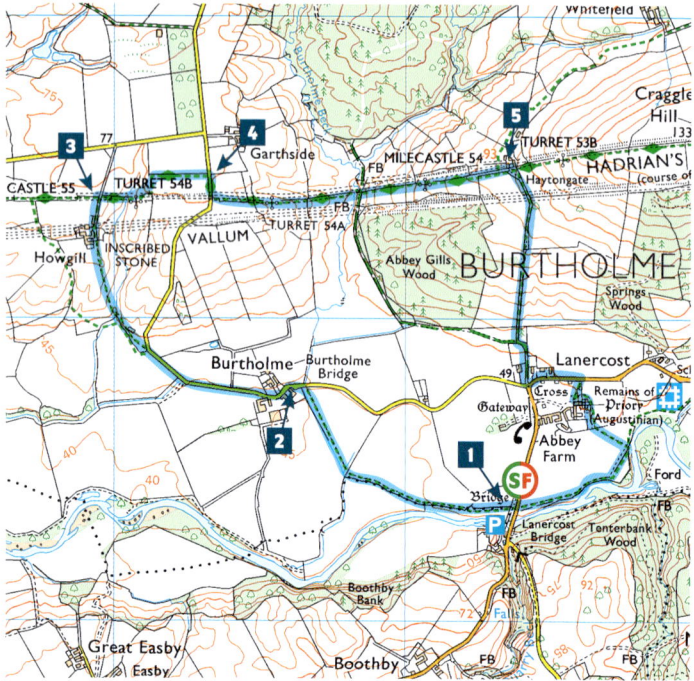

The twin arches of the elegant Lanercost Bridge span the confluence of the Irthing and Quarry Beck. The stature of the bridge reflects its proximity to Naworth Castle, the Earls of Carlisle no doubt seeking to impress travellers.

1 Cross the stone step-stile just before the bridge and walk downstream. Go through the kissing-gate in the hedge right. The path follows the hedge to cross two stiles within an intervening hedge. Continue alongside the open beck. Cross the stile by Burtholme Bridge onto the road.

2 Turn left along the road, passing through **Burtholme** farmstead. Where the road starts to bend and rise to the right take the second footpath signposted 'Howgill' via a rickety stile. Pass a pond, go through a rickety gate, and climb the pasture bank onto an open track which leads through a gate to

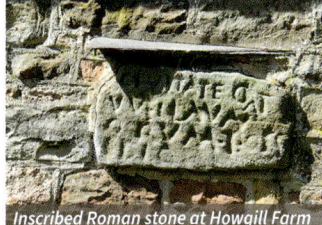
Inscribed Roman stone at Howgill Farm

ⓘ *The first detailed treatise to Hadrian's Wall was written by John Collingwood Bruce in 1863. Still in publication, the current edition of the* Handbook to the Roman Wall *is known affectionately as 'the purple brick'.*

the right of the whitewashed **Howgill** farmhouse.

In the yard behind the farmhouse, set into a low sandstone building, you can find a roughly inscribed Roman stone under a fragment of slate. This records repairs to the Roman Wall in the 4th century by

the Catuvellauni, a native British tribe from southern Britain.

3 100m beyond the farm buildings find facing kissing-gates either side of the farm track. This is Hadrian's Wall Path National Trail which follows the precise course of the Roman Wall. Turn right and follow the field

Lanercost Priory from Haytongate

> (i) *In 1599 antiquarian William Camden visited Hadrian's Wall, saying, 'Verily I have seene the tract of it over the high pitches and steep descents of hills, wonderfully rising and falling.'*

boundary along a partially flagged path through the dip. Keep beside the left-hand fence and exit via further kissing-gates onto the road.

4 Turn right signed 'Banks' and after 150m turn left through a kissing-gate. Hold to the obvious line of

the National Trail by kissing-gates to cross **Burtholme Beck** footbridge and an access track. Ascend pasture by mature trees, passing the invisible site of Milecastle 54. At a kissing-gate enter a fenced passage leading to **Haytongate**.

5 Leave the National Trail at this point. Turn right and follow the access road down to the Lanercost road. Bear left along the footway. To the right the boundary walls of the Priory Garth (the field in front of the church) are built entirely of Roman Wall stone. Enter the Priory Garth at

Lanercost Priory

Lanercost Priory

Lanercost Priory was founded by Robert de Vaux, Baron of Gilsland, around 1170 to house Augustinian canons. It remains a place of peace and quiet reflection. The name Lanercost hints at native/Welsh origins, being a reference to 'church land'. Not surprisingly the priory's constructors borrowed some of the ready-made masonry from the Roman Wall on the ridge above. The beautiful parish church is of cathedral-size proportions. The peaceful priory ruins, beside the part-ruined Dacre Hall, are cared for by English Heritage (www.english-heritage.org.uk).

Looking south from Howgill Farm

the hand-gate and follow the foot-path towards the stump of a preaching cross. Turn left via hand-gates through the graveyard bounding the priory ruins. Entering open pasture bear half-left to reach the banks of the **River Irthing**. Turn right and follow the riverside pasture to a kissing-gate and cross the road into the picnic site.

ⓘ *The first 19th-century restoration of Hadrian's Wall was by John Clayton of Chesters House. The characteristic turf-topped sections of drystone wall were reconstructed under his instructions.*

▬ To shorten

After crossing the footbridge over Burtholme Beck, follow the lane right beside Abbey Gills Wood, avoiding further ascent to reach the Lanercost road, saving 20min.

Bluebells in Combcrag Wood

WALK 3
Combcrag Gorge

Time: 2¼hr
Distance: 5.5km (3½ miles)
Climb: 140m

Discover the hidden beauty of the Irthing and a wild wooded gorge

Start/finish	*Banks Turret (Turret 52A)*
Locate	*CA8 2JJ ///crossings.imitate.paddle*
Cafes/pubs	*Lanercost tea room (off route), refreshment cabin near Combcrag Wood*
Transport	*No buses*
Parking	*Banks Turret English Heritage car park (fee)*
Toilets	*Portaloo at Coombe Crag Farm*

This unusual walk follows the shy valley of the River Irthing through pastures and woods to explore a dramatic gorge. From Wallholme the walk follows a long-established footpath carpeted with bluebells in May. The return is along the line of the Roman Wall with some interesting turrets to investigate.

Path through wood anemones below Banks

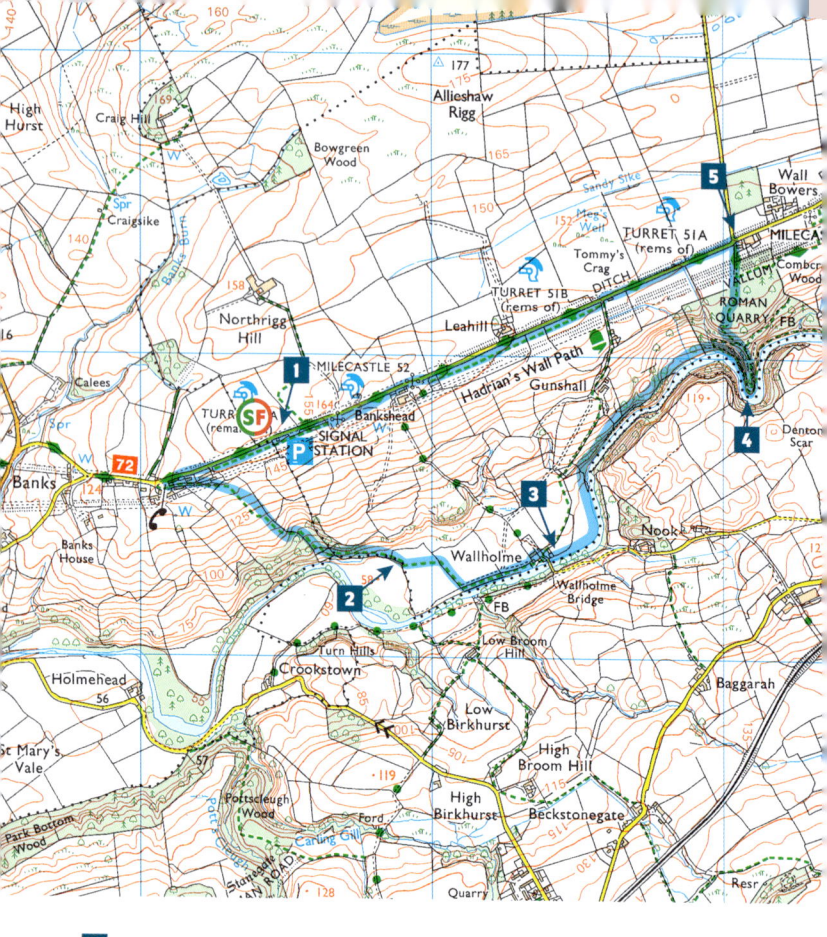

1 Walk west by the remnant Roman Wall and turret then turn through a small gate, along a narrow fenced passage to a hand-gate onto the road to the hamlet of **Banks**. Pass the cottages, turning left by the parish notice board, then left again to follow the farm access lane. Watch for a yellow footpath waymark directing you through a galvanised gate into the pasture field. Descend with the fence left, and as the slope steepens keep to the edge, contouring left at mature trees to reach a stile. Cross the stile and follow the waymark post down to a stile leading to open woodland. This woodland is resplendent with bluebells and wild garlic in spring and early summer. The path opens up, crossing a stile into pasture.

2 As the adjacent hedge curves away, bear across the open field to a stile in the hedge. Turn right and follow the hedge to a kissing-gate and onto a footpath between a fence and the wild bank of the **River Irthing**. Where the path ends at a kissing-gate, pass to the left of **Wallholme** farmhouse through the farmyard.

3 Turn right towards the access bridge, but before it bear left down to a gate into the meadow. The walk

ⓘ Rudyard Kipling's children's book **Puck of Pook Hill** *is set on Hadrian's Wall, with such quotes as 'Barbarians are all alike' and 'threatened men live long'.*

now follows a footpath strangely not identified on OS maps, but which is waymarked. Follow the river upstream by the impressive flood protection bank of boulders to reach a stile into the wooded gorge, and follow the clear path through the wild wood. After a stile the slope opens up on the left, now beside a fence. Go

Roman quarry cutting at Combcrag

Pike Hill signal station

through a hand-gate and cross slabs to reach a wicket-gate. Ignore the obvious path that breaks up left, and continue ahead, coming down beside river with its bedrock falls.

4 The path makes a sudden rise left, climbing the spine of the **Combcrag** ridge, adorned with pines and redwoods, with an amazing view down into the wooded gorge. The path comes to a rock-cutting made by the Romans quarrying the sandstone on either side of the arête. Go through and at the muddy patch bear up right. The Roman-made path zig-zags up

into the coppice, soon coming beside a wall to be joined by the National Trail from the right. Pass a refreshment cabin and farmhouse to reach the road junction.

5 Turn left up the road, now accompanying the National Trail, soon to encounter Wall Turret 51A. After Crag Cottage at a lane entrance to the left step over the gated wall-stile and follow the roadside wall within the field. The second turret, 51B, can be accessed by a wall-stile on the right. The trail continues over further wall-stiles. Passing Leahill Farm the

Piper Sike (51A) and Leahill Turrets (51B)

Leahill Turret with a portion of the Wall

Set apart along a level road, Turrets 51A and 51B provide a unique opportunity to measure out a Roman third of a mile (333 double steps, ie counting your left leg's marching paces). The modern road runs along the same line as did the Roman Military Way, a supply road, and the frontier was shielded to the south by the vallum banks and ditch, seen down the fields on the left. The turrets were constructed before Hadrian's Wall. In fact the original frontier 'wall' was a turf bank flanking the stone turret.

path runs between two fences and ends at a kissing-gate to rejoin the road a few paces short of the 'lost' site of Milecastle 52. Pass **Bankshead Farm** and go left over a wall-stile, then follow the path to a kissing-gate at **Pike Hill signal station**. From here a narrow path leads back to the car park.

The Roman signalling tower was built two decades before Hadrian's Wall, which explains why it is set askew. It related to the Stanegate Roman road to the south of the River Irthing and was visible from the fort at Chapelburn to the east. Looking south you can see as far as the Lake District.

The peaty River Irthing from the Millennium Footbridge

WALK 4
Birdoswald and Gilsland Spa

Time: 3hr
Distance: 8.5km (5¼ miles)
Climb: 220m

A fabulous rambling walk with showpiece sections of Hadrian's Wall and a pleasing amble through a wooded gorge

Start/finish	Gilsland
Locate	CA8 7AA ///knowledge.casually.character
Cafes/pubs	Birdoswald Roman Fort and House of Meg tea room in Gilsland
Transport	None
Parking	Car park beside Gilsland Primary School (free)
Toilets	Birdoswald Roman site
Warning	Take extra care crossing the train tracks

There are three extraordinary stretches of Roman Wall and the fort of Birdoswald to visit on this easy country walk. The route then explores what remains of a Victorian spa resort before homing in on the best-preserved milecastle on the entire frontier, King's Stables (Milecastle 48).

Looking east along the Roman Wall from Birdoswald

1 Cross the road to join the National Trail at the cattle-grid. At once the track accompanies a length of Roman Wall. The farm access track swings right to run along the base of the north ditch towards **Willowford Farm**. However, the National Trail goes through a kissing-gate then the path is squeezed between the fence and the Wall. Pass through **Turret 48B** and step down off the platform onto the track, then go through the hand-gate opposite the entrance to the farmyard.

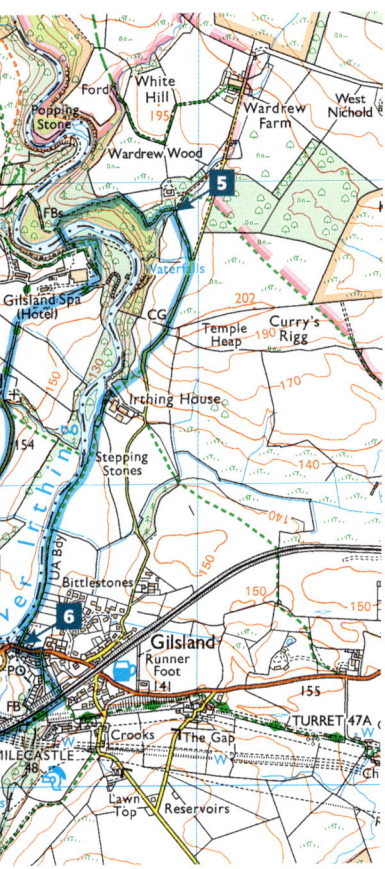

the River Irthing. Cross the fine arched Millennium Footbridge, soaking up the lovely wooded setting. The path slips through a kissing-gate and up flag-stone steps onto the track, climbing right to the top of the bank at **Harrow Scar**. Leave the track, stepping over the low curtain wall of the milecastle to a kissing-gate and an even more handsome stretch of Hadrian's Wall.

The alignment of this section is fascinating as the earlier Hadrianic turf wall ran straight to Birdoswald fort's east gate. But the stone wall, built some 20 years later runs further to the north, and so gained considerable space to expand the civil settlement, which was set on shallow terracing.

3 Nearing the fenced boundary of **Birdoswald Roman Fort** site go through the kissing-gate. A left turn brings you to the English Heritage visitor centre/cafe. The walk turns right and follows the road down past the car park to a gate in the dip. Go through a brief holding pen to a fur-ther gate and cross the pasture, keep-ing left of the obvious hillock, and through a hand-gate. Descend small steps in the wooded dell, then cross the footbridge over Harrow's Beck and go up and through a hand-gate into pasture. Head to a further kissing-gate, circumnavigate a nettle patch and

2 Descend a flight of stone steps beside a fine straight length of Wall. The path levels to arrive at the eastern river buttress of the **Roman bridge**, now some way from the river which has shifted west. A kissing-gate leads along a paved way to the banks of

Willowford meadows from the road leading to Gilsland

keep forward to come beside a wall. Follow the boardwalk rising to a gate onto the road. Turn right to reach a junction.

4 Turn left along the footway past Orchard House, keeping right at a junction with a seat and bearing right again by the parish church to pass the imposing **Gilsland Hall Hotel**. Walk through the hotel car park and join a path that descends to the bridge spanning the lovely River Irthing. You may be able to smell the Spa Well, which you can visit to the right before crossing the bridge. Ascend the cobbled path, climbing right on the old woodland way to **Wardrew House**. At the top left bend, cross a stile onto a path which skirts the garden to reach the access road.

5 Turn right along the access road and cross a further gate then a cattle-grid/footbridge. Keep right and look out for a lichen encrusted footpath sign and fence-stile. Go down the pasture to a hand-gate and straight on through the grounds of Irthing House. Cross a stile into pasture and a further hand-gate (with a seat shielding it from cattle) to come alongside the river once more. The path now runs on enchantingly into **Gilsland**. Turn right, then left after the Bridge Hotel to follow the road directly back to the car park.

6 Turn left and bear right by the community hall, past the children's play area and under the railway. Turn immediately right following the confined path down to the footbridge across **Poltross Burn**, and climbing the steps on the other side to reach **Milecastle 48**. Pass through on a confined path by the railway and cross the two rail tracks, staying ultra-alert as there is a constant flow of trains. The path goes down by gates into pasture, bearing half-left to a simple plank crossing of the ditch to arrive back at the car park.

Known locally as King's Stables, Milecastle 48 this is the best example on Hadrian's Wall, though awkwardly set on a slope. Notice the narrowed north gate and steps that gave access to a walkway around the parapet of the milecastle, not onto the Wall.

Gilsland Spa

Wardrew House

From the late 18th century the old country habit of resorting to sulphur springs for healing all manner of ailments became fashionable with the urban well-to-do. The smelly sulphur spring in the Irthing gorge became popular with visitors like Robbie Burns and Sir Walter Scott and their socialite contemporaries, who lodged at the three-storeyed house called Shaws (now Wardrew House). The arrival of the railway boosted custom, turning this into the significant holiday resort Gilsland Spa.

To shorten

At Waypoint 4 turn right and follow the road back into Gilsland, passing the House of Meg to regain the car park, making a walk of only 4.5km (1¾hr).

Hadrian's Wall weaves through outcrops on Walltown Crags

WALK 5
Nine Nicks of Thirlwall

Start/finish	*Walltown Country Park (Northumberland National Park)*
Locate	*CA8 7JD ///fittingly.snatched.fairness*
Cafes/pubs	*None on route, tea room at Greenhead (1.5km off route)*
Transport	*AD122 bus*
Parking	*Walltown Country Park (fee)*
Toilets	*Walltown Country Park*

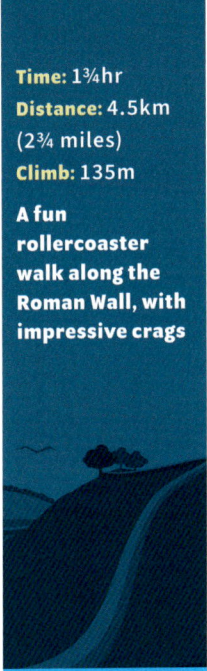

Time: 1¾hr
Distance: 4.5km (2¾ miles)
Climb: 135m

A fun rollercoaster walk along the Roman Wall, with impressive crags

This short walk is full of excitement as it follows the National Trail, which dips and rises along the course of Hadrian's Wall by Walltown Crags, then swings up onto Mucklebank Crags before backtracking with greater ease by the open road to Walltown Farm. A connection with the legend of King Arthur adds some extra intrigue.

Turret 45A was adapted from a signal station

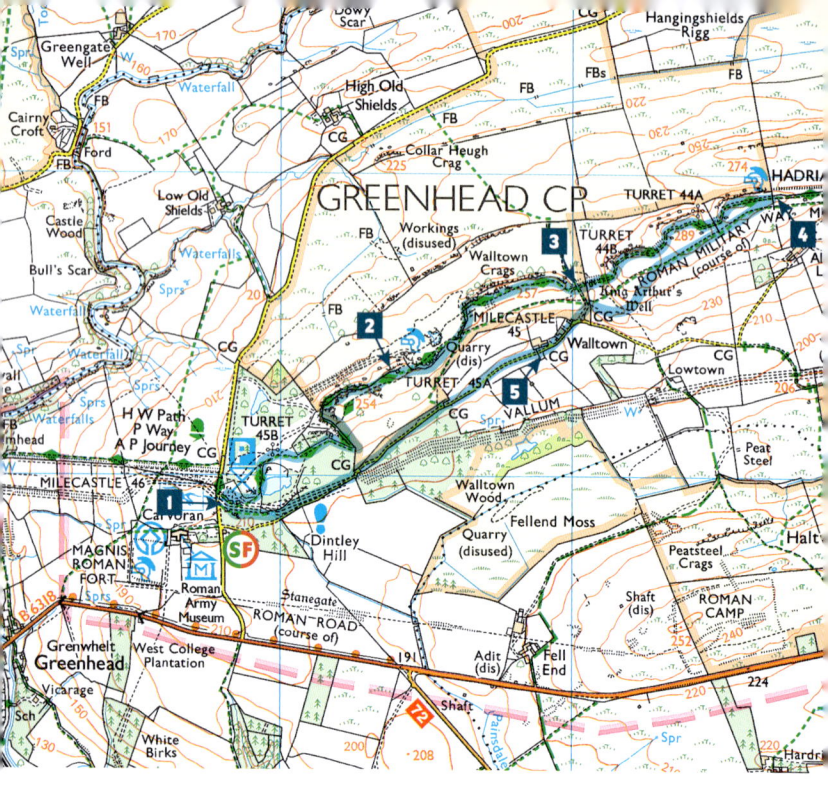

1 From the barrier pass the pond, keeping to the gravel path through the wooded hollow. The path is channelled east towards the tumble of black whinstone rocks and old quarry face, rising to a kissing-gate. Turn left, ascending to reach the remnant Roman Wall. Go right, following the Wall, which craftily found a course through the hard whinstone outcropping. Up to 13 courses high in places, it dips and rises to reach the site of **Turret 45A**.

2 Stay on the National Trial, skirting the even more impressive cliff edge of the eastern quarry. Swinging north, step down to where the Roman Wall resumes at the broken brink of the crags, now little more than the rubble core which diminishes further along **Walltown Crags**. Keep to the ridgetop path which duly swings down to **King Arthur's Well**. The modest spring issuing from rushes in this depression is one of many regional references to the mythical king.

Walltown Farm looking down upon Turret 44B from Mucklebank Crags

3 Cross the farm track and go over a ladder-stile. Climb the steep steps beside the remnant Wall, passing **Turret 44B**. This lookout gave Roman guards a watching brief over the deep nick containing King Arthur's Well, a natural weakness in the Roman frontier defences. The path keeps to the spine of the ridge through successive depressions, crossing **Mucklebank Crags** by a low wall-stile and continuing eastward to reach a field wall

with a ladder-stile, from where there is a lovely long view along the line of the Wall towards Winshield Crags, the highest point on the frontier.

> Before quarrying began there were nine gaps or nicks etched by glacial action through the hard whinstone ridge, long known as the Nine Nicks of Thirlwall. The highest point was Mucklebank Crags, simply meaning 'big slope'.

> ⓘ *Turret 44B is easily missed. Look inside to find door-arch stones nestling in nettles and in the corner, held by a metal brace, a Centurial stone.*

4 Do not cross the ladder-stile. Instead switch acutely right on a very evident pasture path, matching the line of the Roman Military Way. Follow the easy grass path, watching out for a waymark on a stone steering you

The Wall takes a rollercoaster course along the ridge

Quarrying at Walltown

Looking along to Walltown east quarry

There are two former quarries at Walltown. The most easterly remains untouched since quarrymen down-tooled in 1976. Once these quarries were the torrid scene of dust and noise as the hard dolerite (whinstone) was blasted and cut into compact cobble blocks to pave local towns and cities. The cobbling was conveyed on carts down to the railway at Greenhead. Walltown Country Park has been successfully landscaped to soften the harshness of the bare dolerite hollow with native wildflowers and trees, and there is even a maze to explore.

Hadrian's Wall is a solid barrier along the edge of Walltown Crags

half-left down towards the beech-crowned knoll. Go under the beech tree to a low wall-stile to join a track. Turn left by the old water troughs and emerge onto the road by a cattle-grid, passing **Walltown Farm**. The huge farmhouse is sturdily built of Hadrian's Wall rubble blocks.

5 Follow the road across two further cattle-grids and after the last one turn right and go through the hand-gate into the woodland. Keep left beside the road until a flight of steps lead neatly to the bus stop and car park.

To shorten

At Waypoint 3 you can reduce the hilly walk by a good third by bearing right along the farm track in the depression to pass Walltown Farm as described from Waymark 5.

Roman altar at Great Chesters with votive coins

WALK 6
Great Chesters

Time: 2¾hr
Distance: 7.5km (4½ miles)
Climb: 150m

An easy walk on the Wall frontier and a Roman cavalry fort to explore

Start/finish	*Cawfields Quarry*
Locate	*NE49 9PJ ///warns.teaching.slurping*
Cafes/pubs	*Milecastle Inn (off route)*
Transport	*AD122 bus service to Milecastle Inn (15min walk to start)*
Parking	*Cawfields Quarry National Park car park (fee)*
Toilets	*Cawfields car park*

A chance to discover the Roman fort of Great Chesters and the little appreciated section of unspruced-up Roman Wall west to the Nine Nicks of Thirlwall. The return route follows the vallum in its quiet, shallow valley setting.

Blocked west gate of the fort

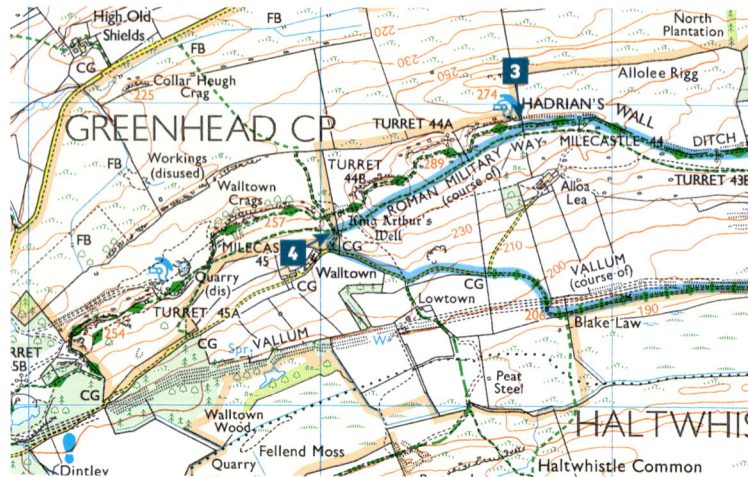

1 Go left from the entrance to the car park, cross the Caw Burn road bridge right and, now in harmony with the National Trail, cross the wall-stile left. Passing **Burnhead cottage** follow the field wall which is set upon the foundations of Hadrian's Wall. Three ladder-stiles in succession lead to the eastern boundary bank of **Great Chesters Roman Fort**.

2 Cross the paddock, passing the fort's sunken arched strongroom (which would have been inside the headquarters building). Follow the track from the north-east corner, accompanying the rubble core of the Wall towards a gate/ladder-stile. Continue by two further ladder-stiles, passing **Cockmount Hill** to enter

woodland, then veer right following the wall core to leave the woods at a ladder-stile. Notice a wooden gate to the right – the left-hand gatepost is a Roman column, possibly from the Great Chesters Roman Fort. From here the wall core periodically appears in the field wall. Pass over **Milecastle 44**, identified by its trench edges where all the good stone was robbed. The ridge swells to cross a ladder-stile.

3 The National Trail continues straight on towards the first of the three crests of Mucklebank Crags but instead bear half-left along the Roman Military Way footpath, which eases down the southern slope of the hill. At a yellow waymark arrow

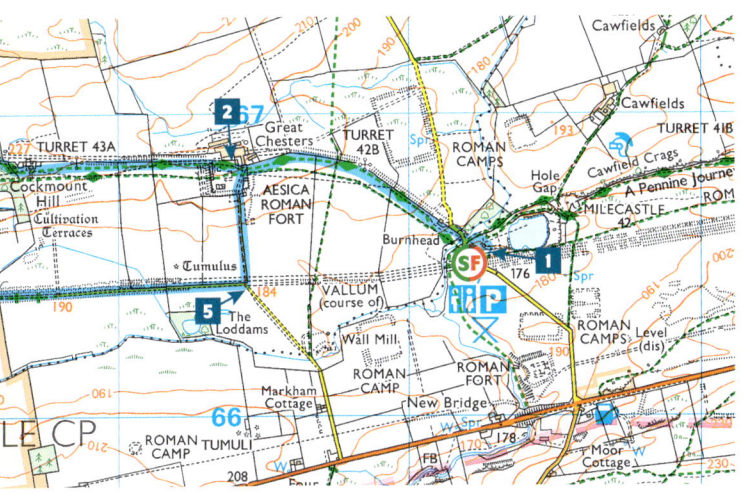

Track along the vallum looking east to Cawfields

on a stone, head down to the beech-crowned knoll. Pass under the branches to reach a low wall-stile to join a track.

4 Turn left towards **Walltown Farm**, but before the farm cut back left over the cattle-grid to join the road. Keep to the road, passing a ruined lime-kiln, and after the next cattle-grid strike right into the cart track marked 'Unsuitable for motor vehicles'. This swings onto the low ridge of **Blake Law**. After the next cattle-grid the track rests upon the southern bank of the vallum, with a broad marshy hollow to the right. A further cattle-grid comes

and goes, and, as a track veers left up to Cockmount Hill, carry straight on along the low road to cross yet another cattle-grid.

5 When the road swings right cross the cattle-grid to the left and follow the farm track, rising to enter the Great Chesters enclosure at a gate. On the right you will see an altar stone, which attracts modern-day votive coin offerings. Continue to join the National Trail, re-crossing the tall ladder-stile on the right short of the farm buildings to retrace your steps to **Cawfields** car park and picnic site.

Great Chesters

Strongroom arch at Great Chesters

Excavated in the 1890s, Great Chesters, called Aesica by the Romans, stands unabashed amid a working farm. It is the most complete Roman cavalry fort in Britain. The turf-covered structures include the strongroom arch of the headquarters building, the exposed southern and western walls, guardhouses, and the western gateway blocked in the late Roman period. As late as the 18th century some of the walls were standing 12ft (3.5m) high. Perhaps Aesica's most intriguing feature was its water supply, a 7 mile-long aqueduct that ran like a serpent from Fond Tom's Pool in Caw Burn, 2 miles as the crow flies from the fort!

WALK 7
Cawfield Crags

Start/finish	Cawfields Quarry
Locate	NE49 9PJ ///warns.teaching.slurping
Pub	Milecastle Inn
Transport	AD122 bus service to Milecastle Inn (15min walk to start)
Parking	Cawfields Quarry National Park car park (fee)
Toilets	Cawfields car park

This walk provides two Roman lines for the price of one: the full complement of Hadrian's Wall in ditches, mortar-bonded Wall and vallum banks, plus the Stanegate or 'stone road', an east/west Roman road from Carlisle to Corbridge in use long before Hadrian's reign.

Time: 1½hr
Distance: 4km (2½ miles)
Climb: 90m

An exciting concentration of Roman Wall features on a compact walk

Looking eastwards from the Wall ditch to the Caw Gap road crossing

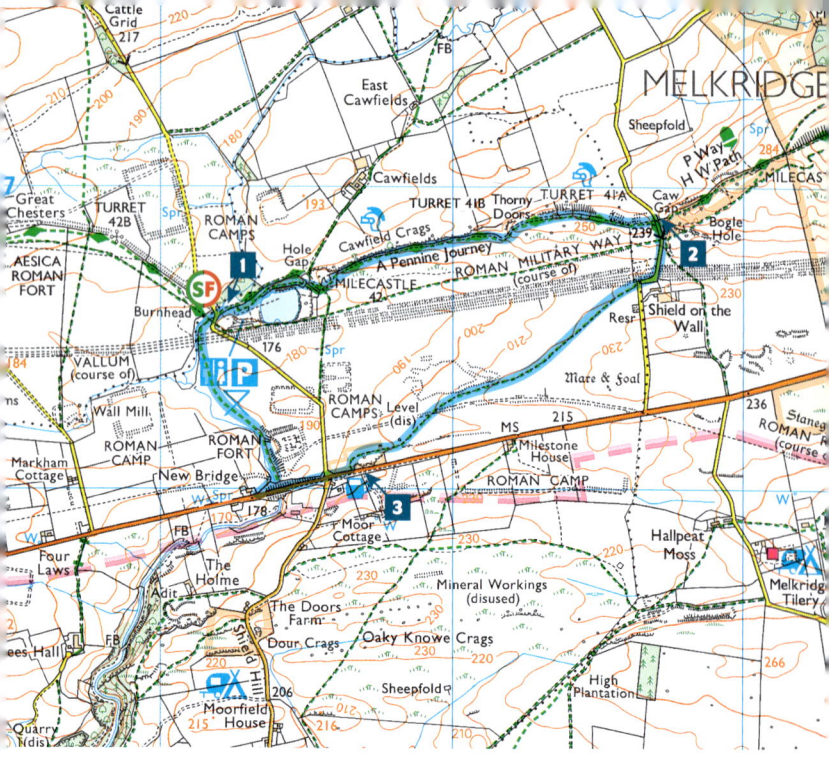

1 Follow the path left of the pool to a hand-gate and bear up to a kissing-gate in **Hole Gap**. From the kissing-gate the walk bears left past Milecastle 42, jauntily set on an awkward slope. Accompany the mortar-bonded Roman Wall snaking easily up the ridge above the tree-clothed **Cawfield Crags**. After a hand-gate set into the wall at Thorny Doors the ridge pitches up with the remnant Wall to cross a stile past Turret 41A to reach a kissing-gate onto the road at **Caw Gap**.

2 Turn right and follow the road down into the dip, crossing the line of the vallum banks and ditch. The road swings sharp right and at the next left bend step over the fence-stile on the right. Take a long diagonal line towards a distant white farmhouse (Lees Hall). The initial path soon dissolves in the rough cattle/sheep pasture notably after the line of sink hollows. As the ground swells crossing turf bank tracks reach the brow of the ridge to come upon the Stanegate Roman road. This was in effect the frontier before

Vallum approaching Shield on the Wall

Hadrian conceived his great wall. Ahead keep to the right of a small limestone quarry. The footpath keeps right, passing below the larger limestone quarry, ending as a track bends to a ladder-stile onto the verge of the 18th-century Military Road (B6318) with the **Milecastle Inn** opposite.

3 Follow the verge right, crossing over the Cawfields road. Keep to the broad verge path down onto the Caw Burn embankment. Cut back with the footpath beside the wall short of a cottage, up over the watercourse then step down to a kissing-gate. Now head upstream on a path that largely follows the track-bed of an old railway that carried the whinstone from Cawfields Quarry down to Haltwhistle. Reach a gate and a stile onto the road and return to the start.

To shorten

At Caw Gap (before Waypoint 2) turn right and cross the first fence-stile on the right, tracing the course of the Roman Military Way for a grassy stroll back down to Hole Gap, saving 1¼ miles (30min).

Roman wall along the brink of Cawfield Crags looking west

The Military Way

There are some really lovely stretches of the Roman Military Way that ran in harmony with the frontier, none better than along the dip slope of Cawfield Crags. The Military Way was used primarily for cavalry and foot soldiers, not carts. It was not part of the original infrastructure of the Wall, but was added when the Antonine Wall in Scotland was abandoned, that is some 60 years after Hadrian's Wall was built. Throughout the frontier's life the Romans used the pre-existing Stanegate to move heavier supplies east/west.

WALK 8
Winshield Crags

Start/finish	*Steel Rigg*
Locate	*NE47 7AN ///respond.snowy.eyelashes*
Cafes/pubs	*Cafe at The Sill (0.75km off route)*
Transport	*AD122 bus service to The Sill visitor centre*
Parking	*Steel Rigg National Park car park, alternative parking at The Sill National Park car park (fee)*
Toilets	*None on route, nearest facilities at The Sill*

Midway along the Roman frontier, this prominent hill has extensive views. After traversing the ridge turn tail by its northern slopes to complete a compact round trip along a quiet country road.

Time: 1½hr
Distance: 5km (3 miles)
Climb: 110m

An exhilarating little climb to stand at the highest point of the frontier

The Sill and Twice Brewed Inn

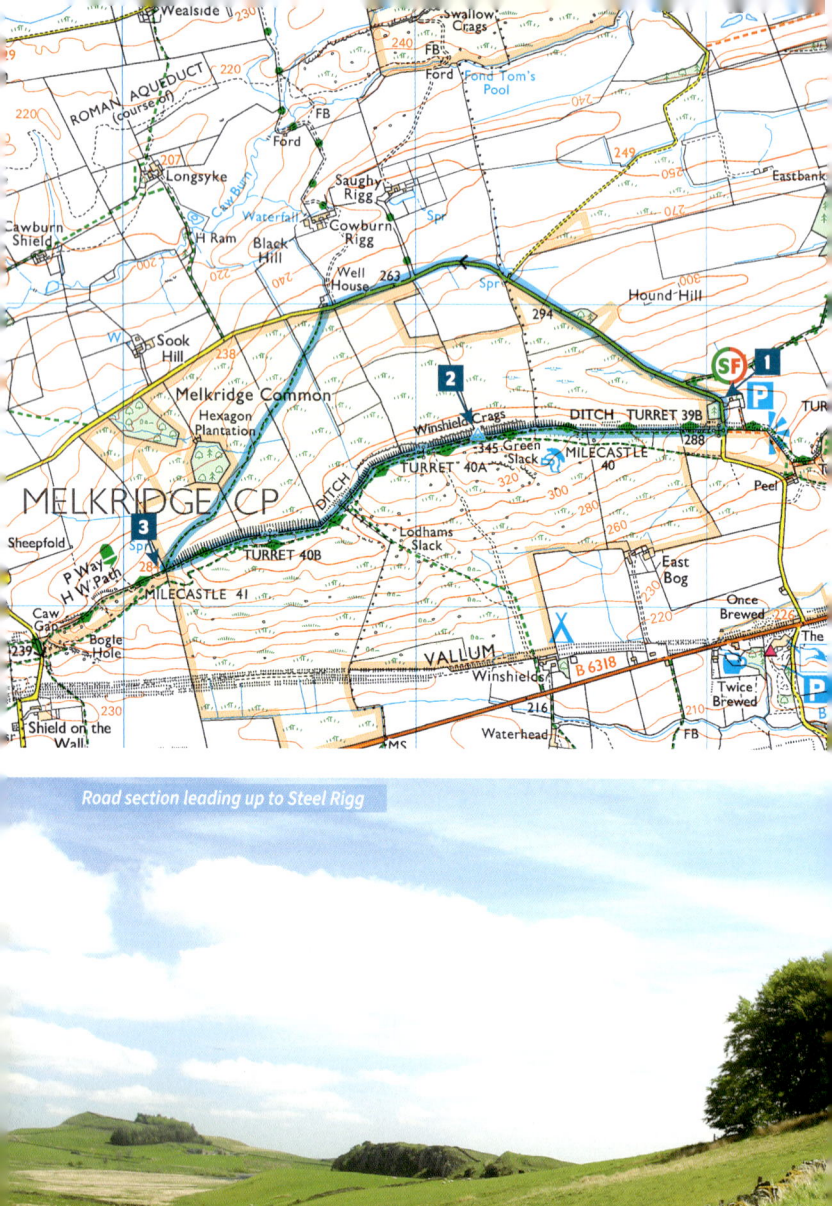

Road section leading up to Steel Rigg

1 Turn left out of the car park, then turn right at the kissing-gate beside the pine copse. The path leads up beside the field wall set upon the foundations of the Roman Wall through a hand-gate. Promptly after the next hand-gate step over the low grass-banked site of **Milecastle 40**. Soon the foundations of the Roman Wall become apparent and then a length of mortared walling up to six courses high, which ends at the OS trig point marking the highest point (345m/1132ft) of **Winshield Crags**.

There are superb views down to The Sill National Park centre at Once Brewed and to the Twice Brewed Inn. Brew is a corruption of 'brow', the inn originally being perched on the second westbound brow (now East Twice Brewed) of the rollercoaster Military Road.

2 Continue west along the ridge with lots of Wallstone to be seen in the adjacent field wall, in sections banked behind. Descend into the **Lodhams Slack** valley and pass through the hand-gate to gain the ridge beyond and descend to another hand-gate.

3 Do not go through the gate. Instead, clamber over the adjacent wall-stile and take aim on a long diagonal line across **Melkridge Common** to the right of Hexagon Plantation. Pass a solitary stone gatepost at the base of a broken wall. Rough pasture takes over and any hint of a path is lost, but keep to the same alignment and soon a ladder-stile is encountered. Cross the stile and carry on the same bearing to the next intervening wall with a ladder-stile, plank across a ditch and fence-stile. Descend to a

fence-stile onto a quiet road at **Well House**. Turn right and follow the road which rises back to **Steel Rigg** car park.

Winshield Crags

Sometimes spelled 'Windshield', reflecting its exposure to wind, the name Winshield suggests 'gorse shieling' (a shieling being a rough summer shelter used by a stockman). The view is superb right around the compass. Looking north you can see the Hopealone telecoms mast and the hills beyond Kielder Water, with the distant whaleback form of The Cheviot to the right. Looking west along the line of the Wall, the Scottish hills are discernible beyond Gillalees Beacon at the left edge of Spadeadam Forest. The southern horizon features Cold Fell overtopping Whitfield Moor, the highest point in the Pennine chain at 893m.

Summit of Winshield Crags

ⓘ *The line of cliffs in the central sector of Hadrian's Wall is formed from intruded volcanic rock sandwiched between beds of sandstone and limestone.*

WALK 9
Sycamore Gap

Start/finish	Steel Rigg
Locate	NE47 7AN ///respond.snowy.eyelashes
Cafes/pubs	Cafe at The Sill (0.75km off route)
Transport	AD122 bus service to The Sill visitor centre
Parking	Steel Rigg National Park car park, alternative parking at The Sill National Park car park (fee)
Toilets	None on the walk, nearest facilities at The Sill

This walk provides two distinct perspectives. First there is a showcase section of the Wall with exciting ups and downs along the Whin Sill ridge and a famous tree in one of the more abrupt nicks. This is followed by a wander through pasture gazing south, away from the steady flow of Wall walkers.

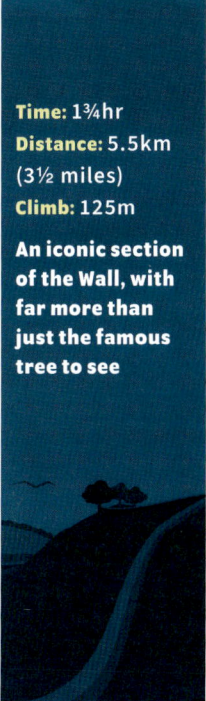

Time: 1¾hr
Distance: 5.5km (3½ miles)
Climb: 125m

An iconic section of the Wall, with far more than just the famous tree to see

Galloway cattle at Steel Rigg

1 Leave the car park along the path that connects with the low drystone section of Roman Wall. Go through the hand-gate and come to the corner viewpoint, always a place to stand and stare at the awe-inspiring cliffs ahead. Descend onto the slabs running through Peel Gap, then climb by stone steps after a squeeze-stile. It's a quick, if stiff, pull up to the top cliffs of **Peel Crags**. Now the path keeps company with the mortar-bonded Roman Wall,

> ⓘ *Along the Peel Crags section of wall you can find a swastika stone on the bottom course towards the end of the level stretch. The swastika once symbolised happiness.*

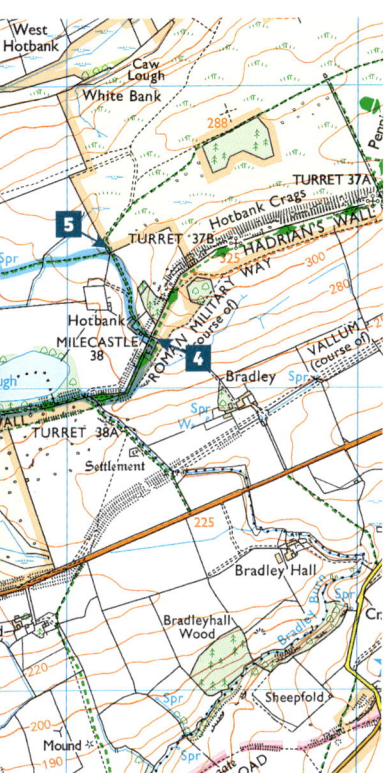

six courses high. The height of the wall declines as it slopes down to a hand-gate in the Cat Stairs nick – a reference to the long-lost native wild cat.

2 From this point the Wall is no more than a trace beside the route. Coming over the next brow, descend to **Milecastle 39** in Castle Nick. The low interior walls are cow byres

from a much later age. Climb the hill, passing traces of shepherds' shelters that once nestled into the burrow of the Wall, then descend steeply to **Sycamore Gap**, with its lone tree standing proud.

Sycamore Gap was made famous by its appearance in the 1991 film *Robin Hood: Prince of Thieves*, starring Kevin Costner. In 2016 the Woodland Trust named the sycamore England's Tree of the Year and it has sustained magnetic appeal ever since.

3 Step over the wall and wind up the eastern bank to come onto the brink of **Highshield Crags**. An exciting stretch follows along the precipitous cliffs, with Crag Lough lying below. There are sheer drops here so take great care if you approach the unguarded edge to peer down on the lake. The path enters a pine wood and weaves down to a hand-gate with the Wall ditch to the left. Go through the hand-gate and cross over the Milking Gap track to the facing hand-gate and continue with the remnant Wall, cornering left to pass around the site of **Milecastle 38**.

4 Do not exit with the National Trail, instead go left by the gate/wall-stile to pass **Hotbank Farm**. From the barn-end metal gate follow a track heading

Sycamore Gap

north to a ladder-stile, where you turn left to enter a large pasture.

5 The footpath leads on westwards to a stile/metal gate. Continue to a footpath sign where the path swings right and left up to a ladder-stile/gate, then comes beside a wall passing the **Long Side** barn enclosure. Keep ahead alongside the field wall to reach a ladder-stile/gate, and soon pass the rusting **Peatrigg** barn. The path is now a track and duly arrives at a ladder-stile/gate onto the road. Turn left along the lane to complete the walk.

> (i) *Castle Nick, containing Milecastle 39, provides one of the most striking foregrounds for a great Hadrian's Wall photograph.*

Hotbank Farm with Crag Lough behind

Hotbank

The name Hotbank is intriguing – clearly it doesn't refer to a warm slope! Like 'halt' in Haltwhistle, the term 'hot' identifies a small wood and you will see there remains a block of old woodland on the brow above the farm. The adjacent Milecastle 38 was excavated in 1935 and an inscription stone was found with red lettering recording construction by the Second Legion under the governor Aulus Platorius Nepos for Emperor Hadrian and therefore within the period AD122–26. Finds from the now grassed-over site cover the entire 300-year life of Hadrian's Wall.

Chimney, kiln and colourful pots at Errington Reay pottery

WALK 10
Vindolanda and Barcombe Hill

Start/finish	*Bardon Mill railway station*
Locate	*NE47 7HU ///condense.impose.liked*
Cafes/pubs	*Bardon Mill tea room, Bowes Hotel and Vindolanda (entry fee)*
Transport	*Tyne Valley Line regular rail services and the 685 bus, both travel between Carlisle and Newcastle*
Parking	*In village close to the railway station (free)*
Toilets	*Vindolanda*

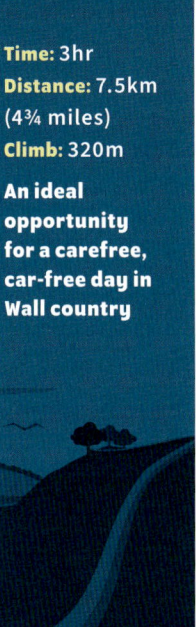

Time: 3hr
Distance: 7.5km (4¾ miles)
Climb: 320m

An ideal opportunity for a carefree, car-free day in Wall country

Arriving by train is a great way to start this walk. From Bardon Mill the route heads up the Chainley Burn valley to visit Vindolanda Roman Fort and museum. The return is over Barcombe Hill, a commanding viewpoint, and Thorngrafton Common.

Bardon Mill old station house and waiting room

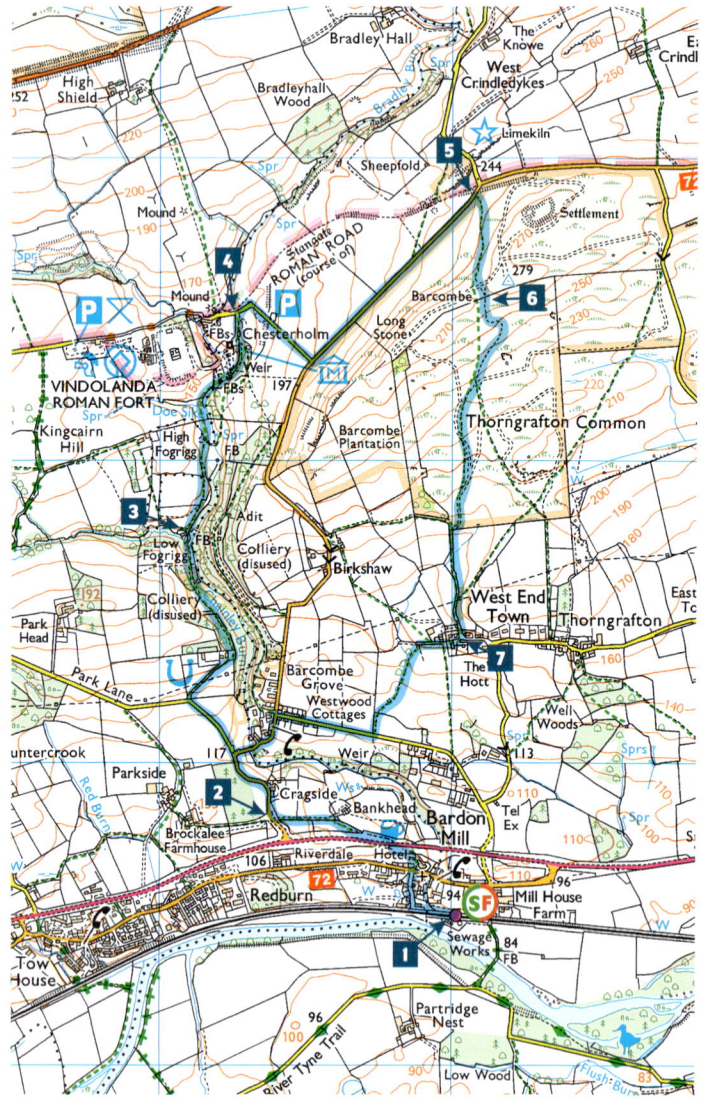

1 From the **station** platform pass the old whitewashed waiting room and station house, following the lane by the green to meet the village street with the village store/tea room. Cross straight over, passing through the yard of Errington Reay pottery with its brick chimneys and array of pots. Leave the car park at the top on a path trending left to cross the A69. This is a busy road so take extra care. Carry on up the corresponding path on the opposite side to a wall and go through an improvised kissing-gate. Follow the wall to a kissing-gate and join the access track from **Bankhead** via a cattle-grid and then through a gate at the minor road.

2 Turn right and follow the quiet road. As it swings right go straight ahead into a road with a brown sign for Hadrian's Wall Tourist Trail destinations and after 300m turn right along the fenced access lane to Cragside Riding School. Go past the car parking and head along the gated track that undulates to a footbridge/ford to pass by **Low Fogrigg cottage** to a gate.

3 The footpath accompanies a fence to a hand-gate and continues. A footbridge down to the right is an optional alternative path. Stay forward, passing the base of a ruin, and descend to a squeeze-stile in a fence, then join a boardwalk via a second fence squeeze below the soil spoil bank of the Vindolanda excavations. The path comes close to **Chainley Burn** and crosses a metal-railed footbridge, with a glimpse of the gardens and museum/visitor centre at **Vindolanda**. The path hugs the fence

Vindolanda Museum at Chesterholm

to the drive, with the museum shop and site entrance down to the left. Pass the Hedley Centre and reach a minor road, on the course of the Stanegate Roman road.

Vindolanda, which means 'white land', is the only fort in Britain with an ongoing programme of excavation, revealing nine distinct phases of construction and occupation. The damp site has ensured that a huge amount of preserved material has been found. Perhaps the most famous are some writing tablets, which give a rare intimate insight into social conversation in Roman times.

4 Turn right to follow the road and at last enjoy a spot of ascent, not too taxing. At the road junction glance up to the skyline above and see a Roman quarry. Turn left at the T-junction and follow the minor road, rising gradually, until 50m short of a road junction you will find a kissing-gate on the right signed 'Thorngrafton'.

5 The path rises easily through the rough pasture of **Barcombe Hill**. Follow the waymark post to a gate in the ridgetop wall.

This is Open Access land and most of the year there is free access to visit the bright white OS trig point up to your left, with its fabulous panorama and the Long Stone to the right. Occasionally this is closed at the discretion of the land

Retired haymaking implements at West End Town

holder, in which case you must stick to the footpath described.

6 Go through the wall gate then adhere to the weaving line of the track trending south down **Thorngrafton Common**, thereby avoiding the dense bracken. The track goes down through green pasture to a gate and into a walled lane. After the next gate/ ladder-stile the lane leads to a cluster of dwellings adapted from the former dairy farm at **West End Town**.

7 Opposite The Bastle House look for the yellow waymark and keep forward over a stile into the gravel yard of a house and cross the lawn to a metal kissing-gate. Keep forward along a passage between walls. Where the wall on the left ends, short of the ash trees, break left and descend the pasture alongside the stream. Go through a gateway, now with an improvised fence on the right, to find a wall step-stile onto a road. Turn right, following

Wayside flowers approaching Westwood

the road past **Westwood Cottages**. At the junction go left, descending through the Chainley Burn valley to reconnect at the junction and retrace the opening leg of the walk.

Barcombe and the Long Stone

Meaning 'treeless hillside', the Barcombe scarp offers a majestic view over the central hilly section of Hadrian's Wall and the impressive course of the Stanegate Roman road, and almost a bird's eye view down upon Vindolanda. High on the hill, the Long Stone is thought to be a colliers' memorial, and was once struck by lightning, hence it is pinned together. Within the Chainley Burn valley there were numerous coal levels, known as adits.

Ladder-stile at King's Wicket, looking to Sewingshields Crags

WALK 11
Housesteads

Start/finish	*Housesteads*
Locate	*NE47 6NN ///revamping.vans.kilowatt*
Cafes/pubs	*National Trust visitor centre cafe at the start and light refreshments in the English Heritage museum close to the fort*
Transport	*AD122 bus service*
Parking	*Housesteads National Park car park (fee)*
Toilets	*By visitor centre*

Time: 3hr
Distance: 7.5km (4¾ miles)
Climb: 160m

One of the showpiece forts on the Roman Wall in a dramatic setting

Lying midway along Hadrian's Wall, Housesteads Roman Fort lies in a fabulous setting high on a dramatic escarpment. This walk allows you to see it in context from all points of the compass, with scenic views and an iconic milecastle. Walk 12 offers a longer version of this walk.

4th-century Knag Burn frontier gate

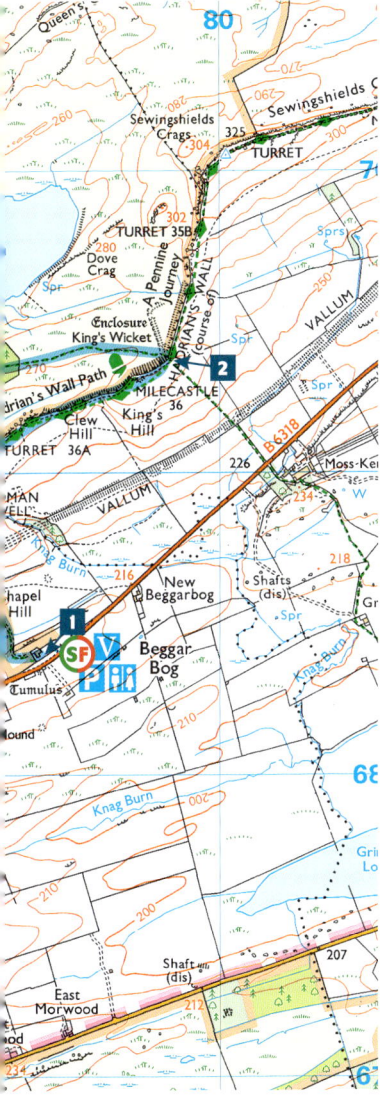

1 Pass through the arch by the cafe and after the kissing-gate follow the gravel trail, down with **Housesteads** and its cultivation terracing prominent ahead. Go through a gate in the dip and rise with the path towards the museum, but short of this break right and pass the southern walls of the fort. Swing round the fort corner and veer half-right with the pasture path leading down into the valley of **Knag Burn**. Go past the wall gate and rise with the mortar-bonded Wall to a wall-stile entering woodland. Go through to a hand-gate and continue now with a drystone field wall close left, clearly built with stones from the Roman Wall. The rollercoaster ridge crosses in turn Kennel Crags, Clew Hill and King's Hill, from where the wall swings down north. Come down to a ladder-stile/hand-gate with **King's Wicket** inscribed on it.

Identified on maps as King's Wicket, Busy Gap was a sneaky way into the Tyne valley used by Moss Troopers, a local euphemism for cattle-rustling Border Reivers, who thus became known as 'Busy Gap Rogues'.

2 Go through and follow the path running to the foot of the bank. Your objective is the small conifer plantation on the brow ahead. At the minor fork keep right and continue to rise up

Looking east from Cuddy's Crags

the damp pasture, taking care not to follow the contouring cattle path. Go through the hand-gate in the middle of the plantation and thread through the conifer trunks to exit at the corresponding hand-gate. Make a short detour to the right as you emerge from the plantation for a good view down on Broomlee Lough. Follow the clear trackway leading west along the ridge top. Soon come to a ladder-stile/gate signed with an acorn to indicate you are crossing the Pennine Way, which leaves the Wall at Rapishaw Gap (see Walk 12).

3 Carry on along the trackway, passing to the left of a double-arched lime-kiln. Pass the remains of a T-shaped bield (a wind-shelter for sheep) with a footpath post and join an open track. Swing left to cross a ladder-stile, keeping to the track to enter the yard of **Hotbank Farm** at a metal gate. Keep forward to a wall-stile and join the National Trail at Milecastle 38.

4 Go immediately left through the kissing-gate and climb the slope beside the emerging Roman Wall which keeps you company all along

Housesteads Roman Fort

Kiln in the south gate bastle at Housesteads

Housesteads Roman Fort is eye-catchingly set on elevated ground. It is the most complete example of a Roman fort in Britain with much of its central internal structure still on show, the latrines and granaries being especially impressive. Terraces on the south-facing slopes were used to grow oats and barley, both in the Roman period and later. The South Gate was adapted as a bastle (fortified farmhouse) in the late 16th century. The ground floor was for stock and was later adapted to include a corn drying kiln.

the ridge of **Hotbank Crags**. The sharp cut of Rapishaw Gap causes the path to veer right. Cross a wall-stile and come up onto **Cuddy's Crags** to admire the famous scenic view of Housesteads Crags at the eastern end. Follow a cobbled path into the depression and up a flight of steps to pass **Milecastle 37**, perhaps the most iconic of all. A kissing-gate gives entry into Housesteads Wood and the path runs on top of the restored wall – the only stretch of the frontier where walkers have always enjoyed the liberty to do this. You can also wind through the woodland itself to minimise your impact on the monument. Go through a kissing-gate on the right to pass down by the western walls of the fort towards the museum where you join the gravel trail back to your start.

(i) Take a look into Milecastle 37, noting especially the semi-arched north gate, with the highest untouched Roman Wall to its left, 13 courses high.

To shorten

At Waypoint 3 bear half-left to accompany the Pennine Way into the pasture dip and over the slabs in the marshy ground. Ascend to the ladder-stile in Rapishaw Gap – shortening the walk by 2km (1½ miles).

Grouse watering stone on Cragend, with Queen's Crags beyond

WALK 12
Sewingshields Crags

CHALLENGE ROUTE

Time: 4hr
Distance: 10.5km (6½ miles)
Climb: 320m

A longer and wonderfully rewarding frontier walk

Start/finish	*Housesteads*
Locate	*NE47 6NN ///revamping.vans.kilowatt*
Cafes/pubs	*National Trust visitor centre cafe at the start and light refreshments in the English Heritage museum by the fort*
Transport	*AD122 bus service*
Parking	*Housesteads National Park car park (fee)*
Toilets	*By visitor centre*

The huge popularity of Housesteads Roman Fort makes a 360-degree walk founded upon its remarkable setting essential. On this route we see the scenic best of the immediate frontier by exploring north in search of more remote scarpland beauty, returning via Sewingshields Crags, possibly the most recognisable viewpoint along the Whin Sill.

Milecastle 37 with its semi-arched gate

1 Pass through the arch by the National Trust cafe and from the kissing-gate follow the gravel pathway that swings down through a gate and angles up towards the English Heritage museum building. Keep up the slope now beside the west wall of the Roman fort to a hand-gate and turn left into **Housesteads Wood**. You may either walk along the top of the actual Roman Wall, with several impressive views down over the craggy edge, or weave through the woodland. Step down to the hand-gate to exit the woodland. The footpath is part of the National Trail and follows the Wall to pass **Milecastle 37** with its semi-arched north gate. To the left of the gate is the tallest section of undisturbed Roman Wall along the frontier, up to 13 courses high. The path takes stone steps down into the depression and rises once more onto **Cuddy's Crags** – be sure to stop at the top of the rise to admire the view east. Continue along the ridge, veering left as the wall abruptly ends at Rapishaw Gap.

2 Go through the hand-gate and clamber over the adjacent ladder-stile, signposted 'Pennine Way'. Strike half-right, descending to cross flagstones in the rush-filled damp depression of **Ridley Common** then rising to a ladder-stile/gate. Keep northwards to another ladder-stile/gate. The turf trail

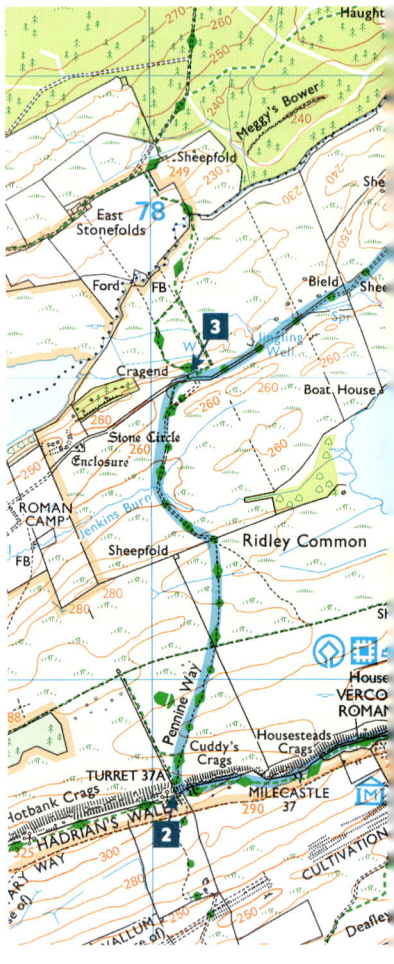

swings left and right passing through the damp hollow of **Jenkins Burn**, then a broad patch of heather to reach a kissing-gate at **Cragend**.

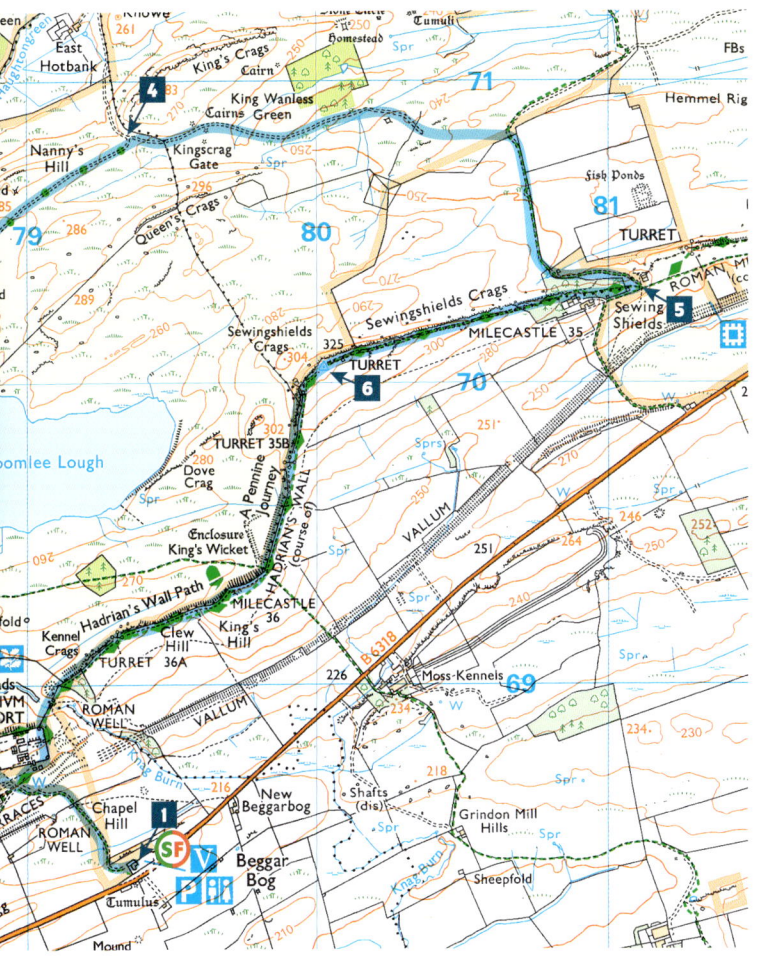

For a brief detour follow the north side of the wall left for 100m to find an interesting stone. A small naturally projecting slab has two cups cut in its top with a connecting groove, to collect water for grouse when this area was an active shooting preserve.

Looking back along Sewingshields Crags from Kings Wicket

3 Go through the gate and turn right to leave the Pennine Way, following the prominent track east. This is the access to East Hotbank, a lonely farmstead beside Haughtongreen Burn. The track passes through a gate, after which glance left to see a stone-fold with a rhododendron on **Nanny's Hill**.

This curious structure has no entry and four wing walls suggesting its function was that of a wind-shelter (bield) for sheep.

4 As the track swings left towards East Hotbank, keep forward along a grassy trod to a ladder-stile (with barbed wire on the attendant Kingscrag Gate). The grassy path continues east and after concrete blocks beside a sink comes onto close-cropped pasture, passing the sycamore copse of **King Wanless Green**. A track becomes once more evident, rising by a small copse of pines and on over sheep pasture to come to a farm track at a cattle-grid. Go right with this track by a further grid, swinging up beneath sycamore woodland to come onto the brow beside a bungalow.

5 Rejoin the course of Hadrian's Wall and the National Trail by turning right to enter woodland by a hand-gate. The path passes to the rear of **Sewingshields Farm** and leaves the wood at a hand-gate, quickly coming

The Whin Sill

Hare Rock under Queen's Crags

The captivating final eastern rise of the Whin Sill scarp has developed an aura of its own in folklore. According to legend it is the last resting place of King Arthur and his army, hence King's Crags and Queen's Crags to the north. The view directly after the trig point is breathtaking, westwards along the Whin Sill scarp following the magical course of Hadrian's Wall to the Nine Nicks of Thirlwall.

upon low sections of Hadrian's Wall. The ascent is very gentle, past a post-Roman stone burial cist, the remains of Milecastle 35 and later Turret 35A.

This section shows the brinkmanship of those building the wall along the edge of the sheer cliff formed by the Whin Sill. The OS trig pillar is not quite at the highest point out of respect for the archaeology.

6 The trail descends beside the field wall, coming down to a hand-gate before rising onto **King's Hill**. Stay with the wall via two quick dips, crossing Clew Hill and Kennel Crags to a

hand-gate into woodland, exiting at a wall-stile to follow the reconstructed Roman Wall to **Knag Burn**. Keep half-left on a path that skirts the walls of **Housesteads** to regain the gravel path from the museum and retrace your opening steps.

ⓘ *The Knag Burn gate was presumably a customs post installed in the 4th century when the north gate of Housesteads went out of commission.*

Walkers heading west from Limestone Corner

WALK 13
Limestone Corner

Start/finish	*Brocolitia*
Locate	*NE46 4DB ///damp.perused.someone*
Cafes/pubs	*None on route, seasonal tea room at Simonburn (off route)*
Transport	*AD122 bus service*
Parking	*Brocolitia National Park car park (fee)*
Toilets	*No public toilets on route*

Time: 2½hr
Distance: 6.5km (4 miles)
Climb: 100m

A fairly level outing to reach the northernmost point on the frontier

A fabulously scenic, elevated stretch of the National Trail offers a reasonably level walk with extensive views up the North Tyne, looping back via a minor road and pasture. At the start or the end of your walk visit the remains of the Temple of Mithras with its replica altars.

Partially cut north ditch at Limestone Corner

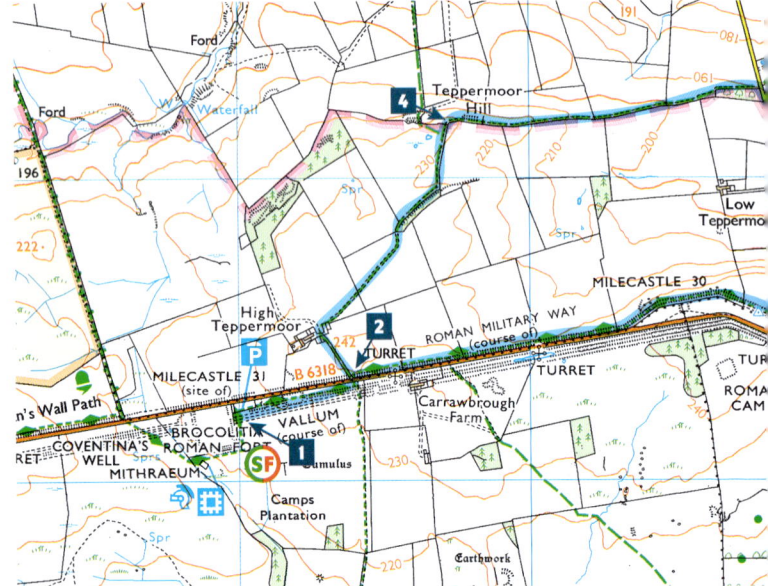

1 Join the National Trail heading east through the sheep pasture parallel with the road to reach a step-stile. Veer left to cross the Military Road (B6318) into the entrance to **High Teppermoor Farm**.

2 Promptly cross the fence-stile to the right to accompany the upcast mound of the Wall's north ditch by a sequence of ladder-stiles. Eventually reach the northernmost point on the Roman frontier, the distinctive boulder-strewn feature known as Limestone Corner. The trail follows the shallow ditch over a low broken wall. Passing an OS trig

point the wall core is evident. A gentle decline brings stretches of mortar-bonded Wall with gorse fighting for dominance in the adjacent Wall ditch. A wall-stile ends this passage of the walk. A short distance ahead is the Black Carts section of Wall, which includes the substantial Turret 29A.

3 Turn left along the narrow road, a peaceful rural byway with wild flower verges. Pass the entrance to Green Carts (right) then Low Teppermoor (left). As **Sharpley Farm** comes close on your right, find a bridleway sign directing left via a field-gate into a

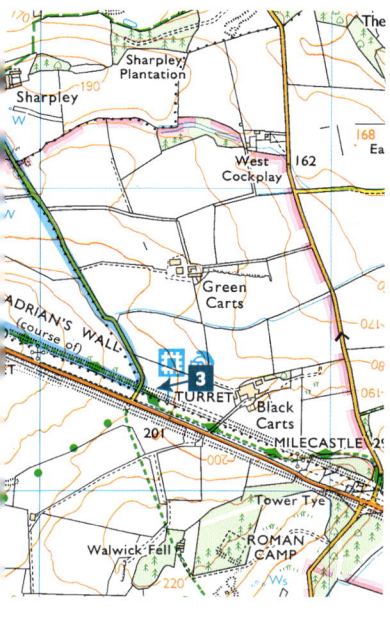

pasture beside woodland. The bridleway leads on, with a wall on the left after the plantation. Go through a gate and at the end of a line of mature trees rise to a gate on **Teppermoor Hill**. To the north Chipchase Castle is prominent down in the North Tyne valley.

4 Rounding a left-hand bend of the wall go through a gate and follow on with a rebuilt wall close, cornering right by the pine wood. Walls funnel the path to a wooden gate then out into the pasture on an evident green track. After a further gate come to **High Teppermoor Farm**. Keep to the right of the light fence used to guide sheep, reach a gate into the access lane and follow this out to the Military Road (B6318). Cross over and retrace your steps to **Brocolitia**.

Mithraeum at Brocolitia Roman Fort

Brocolitia, meaning 'the place of the badger', was one of 16 large forts along Hadrian's Wall and housed about 500 soldiers. All that remain are grass banks. A short distance to the southwest are the remains of a small mithraeum, a temple dedicated to the Roman God Mithras.

Limestone Corner

The stubborn stone at Limestone Corner

In spite of the name the rock at Limestone Corner is actually whinstone (dolerite), though there are limestone outcrops nearby in the woodlands to the south. What is fascinating is the Wall ditch, which was excavated but not completed. Indeed, one stubborn stone has nine failed splitting notches on its top. Clearly the Roman technique employed to break the hard whinstone along fault lines met its match here! Other stones show the distinctive flat faces of the splitting process: this employed wooden wedges which when wetted expanded, an excruciatingly slow process used down the ages in quarrying.

WALK 14
Heavenfield

Time: 3hr
Distance: 8km (5 miles)
Climb: 160m

A wonderfully scenic and historic walk to a battle site

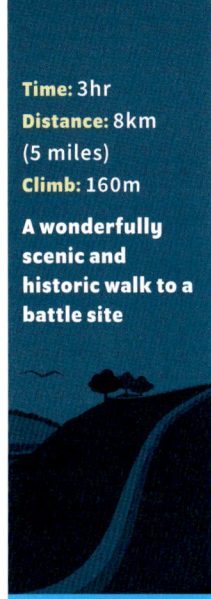

Start/finish	*A6079 layby just north of Wall village*
Locate	*NE46 4DX ///voices.enjoys.respected*
Cafes/pubs	*Riverside tea room at Chollerford and cafe at Chesters Roman site, both off route*
Transport	*AD122 bus service to Wall Garage*
Parking	*Layby north of the village (free)*
Toilets	*On the first green in Wall*

An uphill start is quickly rewarded with fine views which continue throughout the walk, notably at Heavenfield. There is plenty of historical interest, from Iron Age settlements and Roman remains to a 7th-century battlefield.

Bastle cottage facing onto the green in Wall

1 Head along the broad left-hand verge towards the village, coming to the first green short of Wall Garage. Turn left along the road into the centre of the village. Pass by the green with its great tree and swing left by the cast-iron water pump in a stone trough. Pass Stable Cottage, turn left again by the parish church then turn right, passing St Oswald's Cottage with its lintel inscription. The path leads on with the children's swings near left, aiming for a hand-gate into woodland. Go up a steep flight of stone steps. A hand-gate near the top opens to a final rise through bushes onto the ramparts of a Romano-British **settlement**.

2 Follow yellow arrow waymarks through a gateway and right to a wall-stile with large block steps. Advance with the field boundary on your left, swinging up left by the wood. Leave the track and into a pasture. Go right over a wall-stile into gorse, then out across a rough pasture south-east-wards to a wall-stile into a wood. The path crosses over a boardwalk before exiting by a wall-stile into sheep pasture.

Look down to the right over a water trough to see the curved bank and ditch of an Iron Age fort, with a view across the North Tyne to Warden Hill, crowned with a similar fort.

Continue south-east, heading towards a coppice. Pass through wall-stiles into a lane, turning right then left to the public road leading through **Fallowfield Farm**, with the main farm-house to the right. Once the centre of a lead mining community, this is now a quiet hilltop steading.

3 Turn left and at the end of the barns find a bridle track signposted 'Salmonswell' right. Follow this by Fallowfield Cottage and through a broad metal gate, advancing along an open track, passing a tumulus (right).

View of Warden Hill across the North Tyne

Written Crag

Watch for the first metal gate left (way-mark post), and go through it onto a bridleway track, then through a gate to pass pine-fringed Square Wood. Reach a bare limestone outcropping which extends north as a shallow scarp known as **Written Crag**, a major source of Roman building stone.

4 The track dips to go through a metal gate. As the bridle-path swings left observe a patch of gorse in front of a lightly fenced shaft, part of the Red Burn lead mine. Follow waymark posts with yellow arrows guiding left by a fence-stile up the shallow bank onto the bare limestone bedrock. Pass a solitary sandstone erratic, advancing to a broad wooden field-gate, then after the mass of stone rubble go through the hand-gate beside the wall onto a minor road. Go right, following the road to the junction with the Military Road (B6318). Cross carefully to the layby with a chunky wooden cross marking the **Battle of Heavenfield**.

5 Continue straight ahead to visit St Oswald's Church, then backtrack and follow the National Trail west, passing the invisible site of Turret 25B. This is where Oswald, Christian King of Northumbria, is said to have gathered his forces before engaging in battle against the native British tribes. The trail passes an ancient oak and slips through light woodland to a stile entering pasture. Descend to a ladder-stile and follow the field

Heavenfield

Datestone and sundial on St Oswald's Church

The hilltop church of St Oswald at Heavenfield, built in 1737 (see date on sundial), is set amongst a shelter of trees. Benches on the north side provide the perfect place to relax and consider the long view up the North Tyne to Redesdale and the Cheviot Hills some 50km distant, with the Scottish border beyond. Inside the church you will find a large Roman altar and in the anteroom there is an impressive exhibition describing various regional saints and the 7th-century battle said to have taken place here, identified on the OS map as 'Heaven Field 663'. The 97-mile St Oswald's Way long-distance path starts here and leads to Holy Island off the coast.

edge to a green hand-gate to cross the Military Road to a step-stile opposite. Step down into pasture to visit the **Planetrees** section of Roman Wall seen in the pasture ahead.

That this section survived is down to William Hutton who walked from Birmingham to the Wall in 1804 and beseeched the farmer, Mr Tulip, to desist from thieving the stone as it was of historic importance. Hutton must have been a powerfully convincing chap as the Wall remains

awkwardly in the middle of the field, a rubbing place for cattle down the years.

6 The trail descends via a ladder-stile through woodland to reach a minor road. Turn left to return to the layby.

ⓘ Within the Romano-British settlement above Wall you can see the foundations of round houses in the open space. They are stone rimmed and eight strides wide.

Halton church's topiary pig

WALK 15
Portgate and Halton

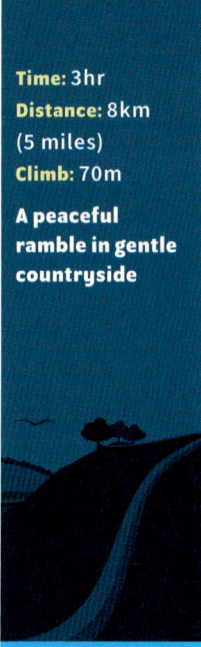

Time: 3hr
Distance: 8km (5 miles)
Climb: 70m

A peaceful ramble in gentle countryside

Start/finish	A68/Military Road (B6318) roundabout at Portgate, near Corbridge
Locate	NE45 5QB ///smuggled.fiction.stepping
Cafes/pubs	Errington Coffee House, plus a selection of eating places in Corbridge (off route)
Transport	None
Parking	Coffee House (seek permission) and in road entry to the former garage site east of the roundabout (free)
Toilets	Errington Coffee House

This is an enchanting ramble with some interesting heritage, including a stately home with a tower. The second half of the walk crosses an open common then weaves through a gorgeous birchwood.

Ornate gateway at Onnum Roman Fort

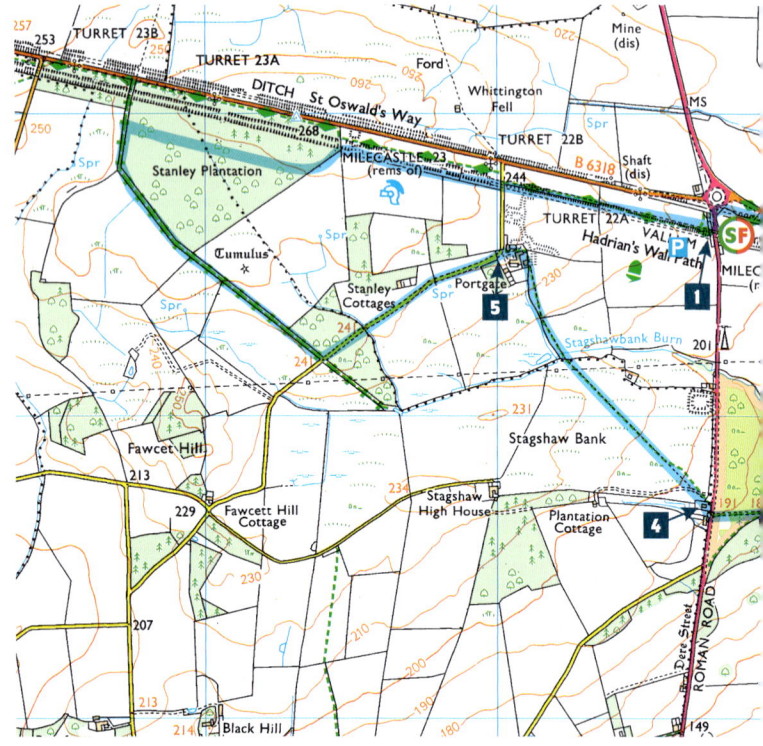

1 Follow Hadrian's Wall Path across the busy A68 heading east. A fingerpost gives the distance to the endpoints of the trail: Bowness-on-Solway 59 miles and Segedunum (Wallsend) 25 miles. The grass path leads to a stile that steps down into the pasture. Follow the roadside wall east, with evidence of the odd Roman Wall squared rubble stone. Pass by a gate/stile and soon veer half-right as

indicated to a ladder-stile at the right-hand corner of a wood over Fence Burn. The path rises beside the wood

> ⓘ *Onnum Roman Fort straddles the Military Road (B6318) with its east and west gates matching the line of the modern road, as it projected north of Hadrian's Wall.*

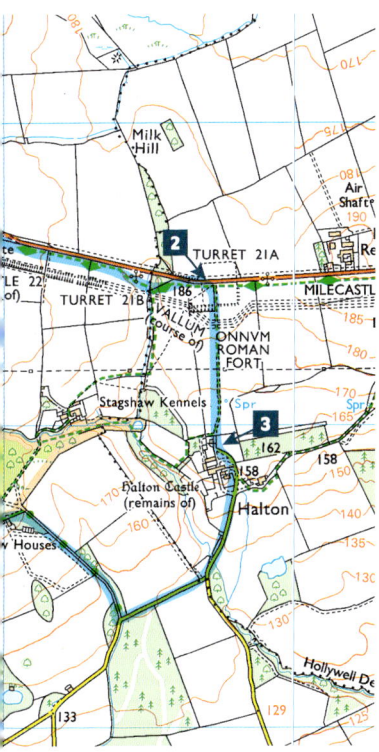

of the fort evident as a shallow ditch on the right. The parkland drive goes down and through the hand-gate beside a cattle-grid, passing a bungalow lodge.

3 Keep with the road left of the tall hedge and after the pond access arrive below Halton parish church. Close to the west wall of the church is a topiary yew pig from where there is a fine view of Halton Castle. Follow the road down to the junction with a brown English Heritage sign for Aydon Castle straight on. Bear right here and where the road bends left, go right along a lane signposted 'Low Houses'. The stony lane rises to where a terrace of houses becomes visible through the trees at the top. Here bear left to pass **Low Houses** and onto the A68 main road facing Planting House, formerly the Fox & Hounds pub. Cross to the broader verge, passing the Old Smithy to an entrance with a cattle-grid, short of the parking layby.

to rejoin the roadside wall to a ladder-stile to enter the parkland space which hides the foundations of **Onnum Roman Fort** (Halton Chesters).

2 Walk to the ornate gateway and go right with the open roadway. Originally built as an infantry fort Onnum was extended for cavalry, with a dozen barrack blocks. After the third tree see the southern edge

4 Avoid the cattle-grid by crossing the stile next to the Stagshaw Bank information panel, signposted 'Portgate' (the farm, not the Errington roundabout). Follow the open road only as far as the pair of pines and bear right, skirting round the gorse to aim across the open grassland of **Stagshaw Bank** between the pylons on a diminishing grass track, heading

Errington Coffee House at Portgate

> **(i) The great open space of Stagshaw Bank was the site of a regional livestock fair spanning seven centuries from 1204, where drovers converged at Whitsuntide and Midsummer.**

for Portgate Farm on the horizon. Keep left of the small wind turbine to find a hand-gate in a wall left of the rhodo-dendrons. Cross the flagstones over Stagshawbank Burn, rising beside a fence and gateway to reach and go over a ladder-stile beyond the barns. This leads by the barns and sandstone cottage to an open road at **Portgate Farm**.

5 Turn left through the gate and follow the open road through the pasture past Stanley Cottages. After the next gate the road is flanked by woodland and a lane branches right. Follow this peaceful greenway until, short of the Military Road (B6318), you find the re-routed National Trail signed right into **Stanley Plantation** over a broken wall. This passage is a sheer delight, the winding path leading through birch, bilberry and heather. The path comes by a replanted section to reach a gate into pasture. Go left with the wall to a hand-gate, with the vallum ditch ahead, partially wrapped in gorse. Keep immediately right by a second hand-gate and follow the fence by two gates to a minor road. Turn left and quickly right with

Beautiful birch woodland at Stanley Plantation

the National Trail by the green gate/ladder-stile and two further such stiles to reach the Coffee House and Portgate roundabout.

Portgate, meaning 'market way', marks the site of an impressive Roman gate through which went a road (the modern-day A68) constructed some 50 years before Hadrian's Wall. Later known as Dere Street, it connected York (Eboracum) with Melrose (Trimontium) and all points north.

To shorten

The walk can be shortened at Waypoint 5 by turning right at Portgate Farm and following the gated road to where the National Trail crosses. Then go right by a ladder-stile to follow the vallum back to Portgate, a walk of 6.5km, saving 40min.

SHORT WALKS HADRIAN'S WALL

USEFUL INFORMATION

Tourist information

Hadrian's Wall Country www.hadrianswallcountry.co.uk

Visit Northumberland www.visitnorthumberland.com

English Heritage www.english-heritage.org.uk

Heart of Hadrian's Wall Tourism Association www.heartofhadrianswall.com

England's North East www.englandsnortheast.co.uk

Travel

www.traveline.info

Bus travel www.gonortheast.co.uk

Rail travel www.northernrailway.co.uk

Tyne Valley Community Rail Partnership www.tvcrp.org.uk

For parking information see www.northumberlandnationalpark.org.uk/visitor-info/car-parks/

Features of the Wall

curtain wall	the actual stone or turf wall that links together the elements of Hadrian's Wall; some sections remain of drystone construction/reconstruction, while other important sections have been mortar-bonded to secure them from the ravages of the climate
fort	military installations used to house up from 500 to 1000 soldiers
Hadrian	Roman Emperor AD117–138, ordered the construction of Hadrian's Wall
milecastles	square or rectangular fortlets placed roughly every Roman mile along the Wall, providing gateways through the curtain
Miltary Way	the road in the frontier system immediately to the south of the curtain wall
Stanegate	a road which facilitated transport from east to west between the Tyne and the Solway; predates Hadrian's Wall
turrets	stone-built towers spaced approximately every one-third of a Roman mile, between each milecastle
vallum	a steep, flat-bottomed ditch with earthen mounds to its north and south, running behind Hadrian's Wall defining the military zone

Printed in Singapore by KHL Printing on responsibly sourced paper

A catalogue record for this book is available from the British Library

Map data

CICERONE

Cicerone Press, Juniper House, Murley Moss, Oxenholme Road, Kendal, Cumbria, LA9 7RL

www.cicerone.co.uk

Updates to this Guide

While every effort is made to ensure the accuracy of guidebooks as they go to print, changes can occur during the lifetime of an edition. Any updates that we know of for this guide will be on the Cicerone website (www.cicerone. co.uk/1157/updates), so please check before planning your trip. We also advise that you check information about transport, accommodation and shops locally. We are always grateful for updates, sent by email to updates@cicerone.co.uk or by post to Cicerone, Juniper House, Murley Moss, Oxenholme Road, Kendal, LA9 7RL.

Register your book: To sign up to receive free updates, special offers and GPX files where available, register your book at www.cicerone.co.uk.